A KING'S C/V

A Brief Autobiography

By

Alan Sloan

Published by New Generation Publishing in 2012

Copyright © Alan Sloan 2012

First Edition

The author asserts the moral right under the Copyright, Designs and Patents Act 1988 to be identified as the author of this work.

All Rights reserved. No part of this publication may be reproduced, stored in a retrieval system or transmitted, in any form or by any means without the prior consent of the author, nor be otherwise circulated in any form of binding or cover other than that which it is published and without a similar condition being imposed on the subsequent purchaser.

www.newgeneration-publishing.com

New Generation **Publishing**

For my children

THE BOOK OF ALAN

To Michael Wolkind QC.

All the best,

King Alan 1st.

Miraculous King of England.
(And probably some other places too!)

Alan

16/5/2018.

A CHILD'S REVENGE IS JUSTICE....................

JUSTICE COMES FROM A KING.

There are many rooms in life, the life of a child has few, yet as the child grows, not only the size of the room changes but the numeracy of them. They become wide and varied with what seems to be many different games being played. Yet the game is always the same it is only the people who are different. The game is TRUTH. The closer you are to the truth, the closer you are to the game and the closer you are to being the game, depending on the level of your truth.

As you grow into adolescents and then into adulthood depending on how much of your truth from childhood you have brought with you gives you levels of insight into "The game".

The only thing is, YOU NEVER KNOW the kind of truth you are.

In the adult world the game incorporates Islam, Catholicism, Protestantism, Judaism, Buddhism and many more. Overseeing it all is the entertainment industry who watch for "The marks" and potential people to crown and usurp in an ongoing self destructive money making market place that is life.

You are not the player in this game you are the played and the Truth. In short you are the watched and very often the accused, with nowhere to be sheltered and nowhere to go for justice. You are alone isolated and gamed in ridicule to poverty. The truth resides within the gutter. The crown, the greatest crown of them all, also resides in the gutter. All you have to do to make the link to the two is walk through the lands of miracles and prophecy. Simple.

Quatrain to Cesar written by Michelle Nostradamus, Solan 1515

With reference to Gog and Magog .... Son and Mason
Alan / Me........ Was Mays son Magog

David / My brother....... Was Gog

PROLOGUE

"THE GAME"

To elaborate, there are seemingly many aspects of it, it involves truth as a major part, prophecy and nobility, leadership, as well as the court jesters and I would think it different for many people depending on your background, what religion you are and what country you come from. From the best of my experience it is predominantly Catholic's who play it and incorporates the greater part of the entertainment industry. You can hear evidence of it in musical references to games gone by and ongoing. You only realise there is even a game going on when it is done to you or you are gamed I should think. Justice does not play a part. There is no justice for the mark. It seems to be, no refusal, no redress and no admission. As I have said the evidence for it even going on comes in lines from songs damning as they are, one are a group called T'Pau The song is called "China in your hand's" One of the lines states "Prophecy for a fantasy, the curse of a living mind" and "We could make the monster live again" A reference to Adolph Hitler, the lines imply that they are helping people to prophecy by making things come true for a fake prophet. It involves a lot of power plays and gross perversion. When it is done to you, you realise how sick it and some of them really are. At it's peak of sickness it involves witchcraft, something I am not going to delve into or meddle with here. But take my word for it, it is going on. You are then a threat to whoever is the existing Head of State in any given country, because you are being given evidence by way of covert power. I was becoming a threat to the Windsor's by definition of power and knowledge of the unknown forces at work. I was unwittingly being given evidence of who I was. They where covertly stealing my life and truth whilst watching me. It is basically a game of truth, you can actually lie and they will make it come true for you, but then I would think you become a player. Something I am not. There are many religions and belief structures on the global market of truth. You can tell the truth anywhere, but there is no greater truth than a miracle. It is the highest echelon of man. You then have to delve into all of the other belief structures. Then you realise or come to a realisation that justice is the key. Everything else is just politics. But to be this or that high raises questions and problems. Questions and problems you have to have the answer to. You can not instigate the game, or so I would think. No one in their right mind would, you are isolated and it is a form of perversion and torture. You are then covertly raped and accused on complaint. I have undergone many set up's and cruel plays over the years, some of which could be deemed coincidental, others have not been. Your game may well be different to mine if it is done to you. But on the proof scale, it is unlikely that a miracle will play it's part in your life. You will be lost in a sea of evidence under an accusation of insanity by an impotent Head of State and a complicit judiciary. The entertainment industry and Catholic's are running amok. You will be dealing with the reality of life and the perversion of the game at the same time. It will drive you close to insanity. You will very soon find out, if you complain about it. You have no one to turn to and nowhere to turn so unbelievable is it and something unbelievable is easy to ridicule. If you fall or fail they will just walk along to the next potential mark I should think. It is this cruel. You will lose your name until you conform into the game and play a part within it. You could go into politics, you could stand on stage and sing like Don Mclaine in American Pie. But one thing you will never, ever be able to do again, is tell the truth about what you are involved in. If you are real and have the values of justice and right, you are forever lost and locked up. It is a way of the constant usurping of authority in any given country, crown and usurp, usurp at the top and crown at the bottom in a perpetual perverted voyeur's game. "And as the King was looking down, the Jester stole his thorny Crown" They would usurp Christ himself. Stealing truth and then saying they are only playing a game. At some point whilst all of this is ongoing. No matter who you are, you will blow a fuse or come unglued and the one thing you will realise is. You don't get to choose. It is a form of kidnapping in the public domain. You are isolated and covertly famous until you find your "Fame" Your proof of who you are in evidence name and life, they have made me MASSIVE. It also entails, at this point in history, having your phones tapped and being watched in your own homes. Justice? Without proof undeniable? There isn't any. A major ongoing and perpetual conspiracy for an awful lot of money and an awful lot of power, unravelled. Personally, I am from a different house than the Windsor's. My lineage goes back through to the house of Beswick and spans over ten centuries in Britain, over a thousand years of ancestry, like many other Protestants in Britain I am sure. Therefore, the Windsor police are not on my side or there for me in any judicial sense, or you, if this is done to you. They will not usurp or investigate their family even for the crime of High Treason or for greater evidence, truth and justice. The mental health "Specialists" are there just in case, it circumnavigates the courts and any embarrassing evidence.

CHAPTER 1

104 Denmark Road, Moss Side, Manchester, England

NOVEMBER 2011

The two mental health workers and two police officers cornered Alan in the dining room of the hostel where he was staying. Wrestling him to the ground and cuffing him, they carted him off in an ambulance to the Mental hospital at Manchester Royal Infirmary.

31 Uppingham Avenue,
Aintree, Liverpool, England 1958.

Samuel Sloan was an engineer with his own engineering business and a fairly well off man. He had served his time as a sheet metal worker in Liverpool eventually starting his own engineering business. He had married Mary Beswick of Liverpool some years earlier. They pulled up outside the new built house on Uppingham Avenue early in 1958. It was a nice area and the new built houses where fairly sort after for the time, semi detached Sefton houses and fairly spacious, three bedrooms with gardens and kitchen a welcome change from the Breck road terraces in Liverpool with shared housing cold water and outside toilets.

Sam got out of the car with May, David and Peter their two sons where in school, they had come to view the house they had ordered built. It was nearly finished. They entered the property and looked around at the building work. Sam went upstairs first and walked into the smallest of the three bedrooms. There was a cupboard built into the room that was over the stairs. He walked up to it and opened the door. To his surprise a little blonde girl around six years of age jumped out laughing and shrieking, ducked past him and ran out of the bedroom door and down the stairs, Sam quickly followed her out of the room and towards the top of the stairs. As he got there, May was on her way up the stairs. Sam said "Where did she go?!" May said "Where did who go?" Sam replied "The little blonde girl, she just jumped out of the cupboard and ran past me down the stairs, you must have seen her" "No, no one ran past me" May replied. It was a story of the little blonde girl who jumped out of the cupboard and disappeared that would go into family history.

Sam would never know that he had just seen over forty years into his own future and seen his own granddaughter from a son who was yet to be born. May would never live long enough to see the granddaughter of six, just as she never shared the vision.

It was soon after that May, Sam, Peter and David moved into the house. They where relatively well off now, the business was doing well and Sam was driving around in a brand new Jaguar car, things where looking good for May and the family. Not to long after the house was paid for. Around a thousand pounds with an eighty pound added option for a garage.

Things where going well and on one warm evening in August 1962 I was conceived and was born on the following 8th March 1963 in Walton hospital Liverpool. My earliest memories would be of The Beatles, I could not have known how big a part they where going to play in my life, my mother and grandmother worked for Brian Epstein the Beatles manager at a shop called Nems music store in Liverpool. Brian Epstein had asked his grandmother "What do you think of the lads

Ada" She replied that they where scruffy and needed a haircut, Brian took it on board, the Beatle hair cut was born soon after, along with the Beatle suits. Little did she know but she had just inspired the better part of a generation to get their hair cut. My eldest brother Peter was a big fan. Peter was eleven years older than me and David was 10 years older. So I was very much the baby. This was something that David had rejected along with me. He had made an attempt on my life whilst I was in my pram. He had to be stopped from smothering me with a pillow. It was to be a benchmark and insight into forthcoming abuse and attacks throughout my life, jealousy, anger and bitterness at my late birth and arrival? Who would know? Who could know why? Peter kept his distance and his own life separate from me for the most part. It was understandable from Peters standpoint, they where different generations. David had the problem and in the isolation of the two of them he didn't mind showing it to me. It became sly and seemingly reasonless as time passed. In the November of 1963, one evening in the living room I became self aware for possibly the first time in my life, though only nine months old and in the living room a vivid memory was etched into me, it was of my mother holding me very close to her and very tight. One of my aunts and my grandmother where in the living room, they where all talking and worried. John F Kennedy had just been shot dead in Dallas Texas. It was a memory I would not forget and possibly my first. I would look back in later life and remember it and my mother clinging to him so. She was a lovely woman who was easy to love. The strength in her four foot eleven frame was astounding and was more than physical. I was to share a bedroom with David. Peter took the small bedroom above the stairs with the cupboard in it.

The house seemed to be nothing but normal at first. The early years of my life where full and happy, I didn't see too much of Samuel, my father due to work commitments, I, for the most part was in bed when he came home.

I would have been around three when my first experience of the paranormal took place. I was lying in bed ready to go sleep, the bed started moving up and down and pretty soon I was being thrown up into the air off the bed at least a foot, arms and legs flailing, hearing the screaming my father burst into the room. I told him as best as I could what had happened. The adult perspective was a nightmare and my father reassured me through my sobs that nothing was there and therefore nothing to worry about. He left the room and closed the door, a minute or so later it happened again with the same result, my father came in a little annoyed this time. He gave the same reassurances and left, with the door slightly open. Even at the age of three I was aware that everything was not alright and it was something I could not see. For the first time in my life God came into the equation. If something I could not see was attacking me, I needed something I could not see to defend myself, that something was God and everything that was to a small child in danger. The room was the second biggest in the house next to the master bedroom and my mother's bedroom. That was the first, for me of a number of paranormal events that where to take place in the house. Other events took place in the smaller of the three bedrooms, people where to hear heavy breathing in the room whilst going to sleep, unnerving to the point of my mother going out to an antiques shop and buying the biggest Bible she could find and placing it on the window ledge in the small bedroom over the stairs. A big old and thick one with clasps on it to keep it closed. It would be worth a pretty penny now.

The next few years went by fairly uneventful. My mother and father had growing arguments that I used to hear whilst he was in bed and my mother always ended up sobbing. I went to sleep many nights with the sound of her crying downstairs. The arguments got a little worse and eventually Sam left the house, another woman was involved. I was six years old. My father came to the house a couple of times after this, but for the most part I did not see him. It was on one of these occasions that my father pulled up outside his house, I was playing outside and he asked me if I wanted to come for a drive, I said "Yes" and got into the Jaguar. We drove into nearby Liverpool and parked in a car park outside what seemed to be a nightclub. My father got out of the car as did I and we both went inside. It was seedy and dark inside with booths and lights on tables, my father took me over to on of the booths away from the bar, when we got there, there where already two other children sitting opposite to where I sat, they where roughly the same age as me, around six or seven. It was quiet as where the children. One of the children was a young girl the other was a boy, I had sat opposite the young girl. Soon after a man came over and looking at the young girl he said "Which one do you want" The young girl looked at me, pointed and said "Him" The other boy immediately said, "No pick me!" I wondered what was going on, why was I here? Who where these people? He just blurted out "She picked me" It was scary, the other boy said "I'll take her" Alan said "I'll kill you" One of the three men came over and said to me "I am going to make you a saint" Alan said "I'll kill you as well" Where was my father? Why had he left me there with them? The little girl then spoke "Would you really kill my dad as well" I said nothing but knew it was her father. What had just happened who where these people? Then my father came back and took me out to the car, once inside my father didn't start it he just turned to me and said "You have to fight now and you have to tell the truth" He said nothing more, started the car and drove off.

CHAPTER 2

Paranormal events whilst I was growing up in the house became normal, being thrown off the bed was just the start of it and always whilst I was alone, to say I was always scared would be wrong, curious maybe. Peter my eldest brother had married and left home by the time I was around eleven and I had moved into the small bedroom above the stairs, it was with some relief from David who had by now began strangulation and or suffocation attempts at various times throughout my childhood, I could have been a clinical psychologist at the age of twelve dealing with his twenty one year old siblings silences, attacks, moods and psychological torture, something that would concern my mother to. Even my friends had stopped calling around to see me further isolating me in my own home. I was dealing with a lot of events both physical and paranormal.

One time whilst I was around eleven I was lying in bed in the same room where the little girl jumped out of the cupboard. My mother and David were working and just before she left the house, my mother shouted up to me to do the dishes and not to leave a mess, then left for work leaving me in the house alone. After some time I arose and went downstairs to get some breakfast, making bacon, egg and tomatoes, after eating it I did what I was told and began to clean up, unbolting the back door and taking out the eggshells and other rubbish. Then, needing milk to put in my tea I went to the front door and unbolted it to enable to get the milk in off the front step. I turned and closed the front door and then froze. I was locked and bolted inside the house, FROM THE INSIDE, an impossibility. Much of what went on happened and stayed local to the house, but if it where possible to be followed by the paranormal or later the miraculous, I was. Maybe I was becoming the miraculous. I had bought my aunt a constable painting whilst on one of the few holidays I had as a child. She had framed it and hung it in the living room, I spent many weekends over there at their house whilst I was younger, on one occasion whilst alone in the house, one evening the painting slid down the wall and broke an ornamental glass clock cover, a little perturbed I started to clean up the glass, as i was doing so, four more plates that where hanging on the walls fell off as well, it shook me up, alone in the house I went and sat in a corner and waited for my aunt and uncle to come home, it looked like I had done it myself, there was glass everywhere, an expensive ornamental clock shattered. Did they believe me? I never really knew, though they said they did, the Constable picture or painting was to play a greater part in my later life.

The nightmare had begun, the paranormal was about to walk hand in hand with the physical. It was generally accepted within the family unit that something was not quite right with the phones, the possibility of phone tapping was discussed, there where clicks on the phone and unusual occurrences,again, it was generally accepted that something was not quite right. The paranormal was me walking to the phone to phone a friend and only to pick it up, say "Hello" without dialling and the friend I was phoning was already on the other end ready to speak, many times. Yet with and or alongside that paranormal aspect of things where the physical clicks of what was believed to be some sort of monitor, it was the sixties and the surveillance techniques where not as good as they are today. But monitoring for what reason? There wasn't one, or one that could be fingered. Once being stopped by the police as a child on a suspected break in at the local shops. Someone had thrown a brick through a shop window and me and two or three friends had walked past the shop some time later and into the police patrol. Names and addresses where taken, when it came to me, there where no records of me living at the property, was it suspicious? In light of everything else, probably a little but to no great worry at that time. You see, when you are walking with the paranormal or the miraculous, the reality of surveillance can sometimes seem paranormal. It is separating the two that can be the problem. Was it because of something my father had done or was doing? No one knew why. As the years went by I left school at sixteen, I was a Protestant, that isn't all I knew by this time, but it was a large part of it.

CHAPTER 3

IMMORTALITY

I spent two years at college and working as an apprentice for my fathers friend before deciding to leave the firm to gain higher qualifications in pipe welding. I had managed to secure a place on a pipe welding course in Port Talbot south Wales, it was government sponsored. I was eighteen now and for the first time I would be leaving home. The paranormal events had for the most part stopped although I was becoming increasingly aware of self, in the being someone sense. I had simply experienced things others had not. It made me different by definition. I put my head down and went to work on the course, welding, it was pipes everyday and after six months I took the relevant tests and passed them all. So, now a certified and insured welder I briefly returned home. I spent some time working for cash in hand, work in Liverpool was still slow, after some time I decided to see if I could get work on the oil rigs, it was the early 1980's and the oilfields where still booming, Great Yarmouth in Norfolk was the rallying point for the gas fields down south. I was twenty years old now and when a friend suggested travelling to Great Yarmouth to look for work offshore I jumped at the chance, we where soon in the car travelling down there, we travelled through the night and as soon as we arrived we went looking for work around the local engineering businesses, on around the third call to a company called Weldco worldwide we where offered work as a fitter and welder respectively. It was a good result, I was told to turn in that evening to work on an offshore barge, my friend was told to return the next day at 8am. That night I worked throughout with another company welder, my friend only lasted two days before returning home. I got a flat in Great Yarmouth and carried on working, the money was good as was the experience, but it was still on land and was not offshore. Offshore was what I wanted.

After a couple of weeks I took Friday off and decided to do the rounds of the offshore companies, there was plenty of work around, I decided to try a welding agency called Magnum offshore and as it turned out it was the ex wife of my current boss who was running the company I was already working for. She hired me immediately and I was booked for a flight from the heliport the next morning. It was happening so fast and so easy.

The next morning I awoke early and the taxi arrived to take me to the heliport. I flew out to the oil rig and the next thing I knew I was working as a contract welder on a Penrod oil and gas exploration rig in the southern North Sea. It was hard work and the hours where long, twelve hour shifts. I was thrown in at the deep end, it was not just pipe welding, it incorporated all the aspects of engineering from a business point of view and I was alone on nights, a multi million dollar company, they wanted the job doing right, quickly and first time. Time was money. I managed to keep my head above water and what I did not know I soon learnt, I had to and quickly. My first trip out was around three weeks, as it turned out it was a one off job, luckily before I left the rig I got a glowing reference from Dick Mellor the Conoco company man in charge of the rig. I was out of work now and travelled back to Liverpool and sent my reference back to Penrod in Great Yarmouth and soon got a phone call from Penrod asking me if I was prepared to labour on the rigs until a welding position came up, I said yes and was soon travelling back down to Great Yarmouth to start work. The work was hard, harder and more physically demanding than welding, it got me fit if nothing else, I did all the relevant safety courses and was soon fully qualified, my job title was roustabout. After around eighteen months a welding job opened up and I was offered it, I accepted and nearly doubled my money overnight, it meant a transfer to another rig and different people but I soon settled in, a lot of the crew where from Liverpool and had done the same thing as me travelling to Great Yarmouth for work. Two weeks on and two weeks off, it wasn't a bad life, the money was good as was the time off. My mother was pleased to see me doing so well as where my friends. I was twenty one and the money was going as fast as it was coming. I had never had much in my life and this was mine to spend, single and free, I helped my mother out, but for the rest, I wasn't saving anything as maybe I should have done. I was still young. I was good at my job and there was plenty of work for me. I spent some time living in Great Yarmouth in flats and had a couple of relationships. As the years past things were going well and at the age of twenty seven I was set up on a blind date with the woman I was to marry, Yvonne. She was around twenty five. We moved in together and set up home, in 1989 she fell pregnant and we got married, the pregnancy was planned. Everything seemed to be going well. The paranormal events had all but stopped and I was in permanent employment.

    I went back to work in January 1990 to an out of work rig, they had towed it just off Great Yarmouth and had laid everyone off apart from a skeleton crew, a crew they kept on for maintenance, I was part of it. There was a lot of work to do and rather than the pace of work slowing, it increased. There was a lot of "old" maintenance to do and the rig was tendering for other drilling work. So the work had to be done quickly, stripped and rebuilt, pipe work, walkways, towers and platforms. The work was such that I and another contract welder had been asked to work eighteen hour shifts and I stayed on an extra week. Tired was not the word, around five hours sleep a night. One morning I was sorting out some scrap steel and my mind wandered to the passing of my grandfather some years before, I remembered how upset my mother was, whilst I was thinking about it a robin flew down and landed on my head, we where seven miles offshore and I thought it unusual as we where to far out for it. Although a shy bird it stayed on my head for what seemed like an age and then flew off. It didn't disturb me, though I thought it a little strange.

The deep well tower or raw water tower was next on the agenda to be repaired. It basically went through the main deck and down to the sea to pump salt water back on board to be desalinated and used for rig water, it travelled up and down to the sea on big cogs and when fully out of the water rose around seventy foot above the deck, it could only be worked on around the top of the tower when in position and down into the water. It was in this position whilst the restoration work was taking place. Dennis Wales, a contract welder was working with me as we started to strip off the old and damaged walkway, we where both very tired by now and we where into our third week offshore and the hours where cruel. Standing by the handrail after tea one morning, the robin returned and again landed on my head, I stood motionless as it again got comfortable before flying away a minute or so later. Could it have been a sign of what was about to happen?

My mother was at my aunt's house on the Wirral

she was staying there. They where sisters and where very close, laughing and giggling like schoolgirls. The print of the Constable painting that I had bought for my aunt as a child was hanging back up on the wall in the living room by now. It was three o'clock in the afternoon as Dennis and I left the coffee shop to carry on repair work on the deep well. Dennis climbed up the ten foot or so off the deck to carry on stripping old walkway on one side of the tower with his back to me, Steve Garrod the crane operator was standing outside the crane cab keeping watch. I climbed up onto the tower to carry on burning the other side of the old walkway out. We where both working directly over the sea and above was a mass of pipe work and ultimately water, without safety harnesses or any form of restraint. I stood up to burn an awkward part of the grating out and was standing on two single cross beams with nothing else below except sea and pipe work.

My mother, May, was laughing with Norma her sister in the living room, it was just after three o'clock when the Constable painting slid down the wall and shattered, she stopped laughing and just said "Oh my god Alan" I had leant forward and keeled over, falling into the deep well and what should have been down to certain death. Steve the crane operator had witnessed everything, Dennis was blind sided. Steve ran down from the crane as soon as he had seen it, expecting to see me floating dead in the sea. What he expected and what he saw where two different things altogether. I was lying unconscious on the main deck on the other side of the deep well with a seriously injured back but still onboard and alive. Steve was in disbelief, it was impossible I should have been dead, but I wasn't.

I woke up to the proverbial crowd around me and in agony unable to move, a helicopter medivac had been Called in to the rig from Yarmouth, they stretchered me off the rig and onto the medi vac, the chopper flew me straight into the hospital grounds so bad were my injuries. I spent two weeks in the hospital with no broken bones and just muscle damage, I was very lucky, the gravity of what had happened had not dawned on me just yet. The rig manager came in to see me from the land office and questioned me as to what had happened, I could not explain it, but tried with the words "Somebody up there likes me" The rig manager smiled nervously, I should have been dead. No one could figure out what had actually happened. The rig manager left as if shaking his head in disbelief. I was discharged to a heavily pregnant Yvonne and a month later on 28th February 1990 Jack Sloan was born a beautiful healthy bouncing boy. I had a wife and a son now and as bad as my injuries were I had to get back to work. Once back on the rig I found out all that had happened whilst I was in hospital, one of the first people I saw was Steve the crane operator, he was perplexed and unsure, he was motioning with his arms, "What happened?, what happened!?, the accident investigators thought we where lying to them when we told them what we had witnessed and see happen" I just shrugged my shoulders not knowing what to say, Steve walked away shaking his head saying "I'll never understand it!" I was twenty seven years of age and had reached immortality.

CHAPTER 4

Swindled out of my inheritance

We had moved into a detached house on the Wirral with Jack and the marriage was already on the rocks. Jack had already been born. My mother's cancer had returned, she was no longer clear and in ill health. Yvonne had fallen pregnant again and three weeks before the baby was born my mother was taken into the Marie Curie cancer care hospital in Liverpool for the last time. On 14th August 1992 a beautiful healthy baby girl called Marybeth Sloan was born in Arrowe Park hospital on the Wirral. My mother still failing had held on so she could see the baby before she passed away, the doctors didn't know where she had got her strength from. I took the baby in to see her a few days later. Two days after that on the 21st August 1992 the True Queen of England passed away. She was from the Beswick line of nobility and had lineage going back before the 10th century Britain. It was a noble line with heraldry and a coat of arms she was a daughter and direct descendant of William Beswick of Liverpool, her father and my grandfather. She had written into her will that the house of my birth be shared between me and my brothers and sold immediately. 25% each was to go to me and Peter and 50% to David as the single man and occupant. It was at this time that David's attitude towards me changed and he became a doting loving brother to both me and my children. It would be some years later until I was to find out why. He became tearful, upset and childlike when the matter of selling the house arose, he had not worked for twenty years and it would mean getting a job and mortgage of his own, he could not handle it. He was lazy and a shirker but he was so loving to me and the children now, how could I force him to sell? Peter was also on David's side regarding the sale. He did not want it sold either. A new agreement was drafted up with a solicitor so as to allow David to stay in the house and both I and Peter signed it. This was when David changed his tune, attitude and everything. He was back to his devious sociopath self, it would bring back memories of my childhood friends refusing to call around at the house because of it. It was safe to say the relationship had deteriorated to the point of violence from David again. I had been brow beaten and tricked into signing the new solicitor's document by Peter and David. I was devastated at my mothers passing. Being the youngest had not made it any easier. I continued to visit the house I still had rights to it. David did not upkeep the property and I had various discussions with Peter surrounding David's inability, but to no avail. The years past and my two children grew, I began to get into trouble with my own property, Yvonne had not been paying the mortgage and arrears where mounting up, I needed my birth home sold and my inheritance realised to save my home and marriage, it should have been over £25,000. But Peter and David stonewalled me when the subject came up. They did not and would not offer me the same latitude they offered themselves. I was closer and closer to losing my own home. I spent some time going over to see David at the house to reason with him. It was to no avail. One occasion, before going back to work on the rigs I went to the house to see David and David's long term girlfriend a nurse called Shirley Hawkard was there, they asked me to stay for something to eat and I accepted. I sat in the living room whilst the meal was being cooked in the kitchen by the two of them. Around an hour later I heard a loud crash and assumed that a plate had fallen to the floor and broken, they where laughing a minute or so later and I thought nothing of it. After a few more minutes David came in with my meal on a tray and handed it to me, it was a stew in a bowl. I began to eat it, nearly finishing it I took another spoonful and was shocked to find a large piece of crockery on my spoon. I put the meal down realising what the crash was. They had dropped the stew on the floor smashing the bowl it was in and scooped it up off the floor and fed it to me, broken pieces and all, laughing whilst doing it. I took the tray into the kitchen and saying nothing announced I was leaving, then left the house to go and see the children at their aunts in Walton Liverpool, we where to spend the night there before I returned to work on the rig the next morning. That night my stomach was bad but thinking nothing of it I ignored it. I got up the next morning and got ready for work, the train journey to Yarmouth was six hours and I wasn't looking forward to it feeling as I was. I picked up my heavy bag and left for work on the train. I arrived in London, where I was to change trains. I had a trip on the underground with my heavy bag to Liverpool Street. I slung my bag over my shoulder and set of to the underground, up and down stairs and escalators, the sweat was dripping off me, unusually so. I got to the bottom of the last escalator before the train and was close to collapsing, I had to put my bag down and lean against a wall. I felt a rising in my stomach I could not contain and threw up nearly two pints of blood all over the platform. An ambulance was called and I was rushed to the hospital with internal bleeding. I only just made it passing out through lack of blood on arrival. They gave me a transfusion without realising what had happened. It turned out on examination that I had a split in my gullet due to the crockery meal. David and Shirley had nearly killed me. Had I died no one would have known why. I had to miss another trip at work causing more hardship in the monetary sense.

CHAPTER 5

Beautiful South "Liverpool, Rotterdam, Rome"

Elizabeth Windsor to Paul Burrel butler, after Diana Spencer's death " Be careful, there are forces at work in this country of which we have no knowledge"

Thing's where about to take a turn for the worst on the oil rig, the rig had lost a contract and was "stacked" a few miles off Great Yarmouth. All of the crew had been laid off apart from a small maintenance staff, I was one of them. I had an argument with one of the supervisors and was threatened by him physically. It was not my fault. I was doing my job and went into the office upstairs to discuss it with the rig manager. The situation was not resolved by him and my position, having being threatened was untenable, I had no alternative other than to leave the rig after ten years of service. I informed the land based office of my intention at going to a tribunal over the matter and explained what had happened. It really wasn't my fault, the supervisor had the problem. Something they recognised and awarded me £6,000 compensation but I was still out of work.

Around this time Emily was born on 30 January 1998, another beautiful little healthy baby girl and my second daughter. We now had three children, a failing marriage and mortgage arrears. I needed a job badly, I tried and got into Cammell Laird ship yard in Liverpool, the work was sporadic, two weeks here and there but the money was good, it was around £700 per week on nights if you could get on them. I managed to more often than not so it kept the wolves away from the door for the time being. In between work I spent time at my birth home in Aintree, I would go over there to check on the property, then I was laid off again and it became increasingly obvious we would eventually lose the house. Still trying to appeal to David to sell so I could save my own home I went over to Aintree to discuss it with him yet again, I took my eldest daughter Marybeth who was around six. We arrived and I let myself in, the house was empty, David wasn't even living there, Marybeth immediately ran to explore in the empty house, running up the stairs she disappeared, I stayed downstairs and made a cup of tea, the place was quiet. After a few minutes I heard a shout from upstairs "Daad!" Then it went quiet. Then she shouted again a little louder and longer "Daaaad!" Then quiet again. I knew where she was, she was in the small bedroom hiding. I knew every creak on the stairs and adjusted my footing for silence as I climbed them. She was a lovely loving and giving child. I reached the top of the stairs in silence, and crept toward the open door of the small front bedroom, I peered into the room and she was not in sight, I knew where she was, she was hiding in the built in cupboard over the stairs, I stood motionless waiting for her. Eventually she creaked open the cupboard door and seeing me standing there, she shrieked and jumped out of the cupboard laughing and giggling, running toward me in the doorway, she gave a shoulder dip as I reached out to grab her and ran past me across the landing and down the stairs. For a split second I froze, the hairs on the back of my neck standing on end, my father's vision of the little blonde girl jumping out of the cupboard laughing and shrieking as she ran down the stairs had just come full circle, 40 years later.

I never really discussed this kind of thing with anyone. It was part of, or becoming part of the normality of my life. Phone numbers for work where often passed around amongst the other welders, a lot of it was in Europe and predominantly Holland, the shipyards in Rotterdam and other factories. It was an option I could not afford to ignore and eventually secured a job, travelling over there I began work, I enjoyed working in a different country and the work wasn't any harder, most of the Dutch spoke English so it wasn't too bad. The work never really lasted that long so there where a few trips back to England and then back out to Holland. This particular trip I was working with Mick an Irish man, the agency we where working for had hired us a car and I was driving, we where staying in a house on a housing estate. We used to get home and often go out for a drink to one of the local bars, although money was tight, staying in the house night after night was too much. This particular night Mick did not fancy going out, I had a dodgy stomach but did not fancy staying in the house so decided to go for a pint, I walked maybe two miles to the bar and stayed for no longer than an hour or two, having maybe three drinks. I left the bar and started to walk back to the digs and after a few minutes my stomach started playing up and I needed the toilet, electing to carry on walking as the house wasn't to far I speeded up. Getting on to the estate it was darkening and all of the houses looked the same, it was one of those housing estates where all of the houses and street plans where the same, even the hedgerows where placed similar. By now I was desperate and worried. I could not find the house. I could not wait any longer and thinking it was dark enough I dived into the nearest bushes. It was diarrhoea and I had to take my jeans off to use my "Red underwear" to wipe my backside. Eventually finishing and getting my pants back on I sheepishly emerged from the bushes minus my "Red underwear" More relaxed and with more time to think clearly and see, I looked up and to my surprise realised I was outside the house where we where staying. I walked in to the house and told Mick the story of what had just happened and we both had a good laugh about it.

The work eventually finished and I travelled back home again. Not to long after that "Liverpool, Rotterdam and Rome" by Beautiful South was released and went straight to number one. Listening to my children singing it and listening to it on the radio, they where singing about me, the reference to "Red underwear" was no coincidence and given I was from Liverpool and working in Rotterdam, to me it all made sense Rome was a reference to The Vatican and Cesar. Someone had picked up on the story, whether it was Mick by word of mouth, or by other means I do not know, but it was definitely written about me, of that I was sure.

It was surreal, someone was telling me they knew who I was, or making me famous. Whatever it was, I had been partway crowned and fingered covertly behind my back. You see, the title "Liverpool, Rotterdam, Rome" Had meaning, Liverpool where I was born, Rotterdam, where I was working and Rome, a reference to the quatrain to Cesar or to be more precise me. I had read the quatrain some time earlier like so many people before me. It was written by a 16 century prophet called Michelle Nostradamus, he was a man who reputedly could see into the future and wrote some books about his visions and prophecies in code in 1555 A/D. The books, as is the quatrain to Cesar are still in print today. Was this the beginning of some sort of game or indeed just part of the same covert one? You see, whilst some of you may feel a little flattered at having a song written about you, I personally found it a little bit sinister and invasive. Again I said nothing. So, they had partway crowned me and at some point watched or heard me, perhaps listening I do not know. What did it all mean? To understand what it means you have to listen to another song by a singer called Don Mclean, the song is called "American pie" There are obviously many lines in the song, but as yet the song has never been explained, Don Mclean when asked what it meant, simply said "It means I never have to work again" so popular was it. Within the song is the line, "And as the King was looking down the jester stole his thorny crown" It is a reference to a King and a court jester or joker. They can not be trusted. So rather than singing to and adhering to an existing King they look for others to crown, "They" being the entertainment industry. They are telling you, or Don Mclean is telling us, they would steal the crown of Christ and since jesters do not, or can not wear crowns they crown other people and watch them. So when I say it was a little perturbing and they had part way crowned me covertly, you will understand my justifiable concern at an apparently meaningless pop song, given it was not paranoia and known to me to be about me. How many people knew it was me? Or who knew who I was? It was a direct hit. I spent some time thinking about what could I do about it as well as wondering how closely was I being watched ?, I just did not know, I knew I was famous albeit covertly, very famous if you take the numeracy of all the people listening to the music. I travelled back to Holland for work again. I had not even told Yvonne of the song, whether she knew or not I am unaware, others certainly did. On one occasion an Englishman in a bar came up to me and told me to kill myself, on another a barmaid stated that "They are playing a cruel game with you" and "You are famous"

I was staying in Kinderdyke in Holland with three other welders at a local house, I had my own room the others where sharing. We used to travel to work along the dykes in an old Volkes wagon camper van that one of them had driven over to Holland. One morning as we drove along the dyke road it became very quiet in the van, no one having anything to say. There wasn't a soul around and the fields stretched for miles. All of a sudden the ground erupted with the largest flock of black birds I had ever seen, it undulated for miles and disturbed the driver so eerie was it, my nightmare was about to worsen. Kinderdyke was a small town with a local bar. We spent some time in there after work. One particular night whilst walking the short distance home I became aware of a foul smell and by the time I got back to the digs I was nauseous and the smell was horrendous, on my arrival I questioned the other welders as to what it was, they told me they could not smell anything, I first thought a sewer had broken. It got worse, I was gagging at the overpowering stench, it took on a smell of burning flesh and I felt physically sick. By this time the owner of the house had come in to the dining room, overhearing the discussion he asked what was the matter, I questioned him as to what the smell was, he stated that he could not smell anything either. I told him it was horrendous and it was making me feel quite ill, he was a little disturbed by this as was I, it was as if I was in a huge room with a low ceiling and could not escape the smell wherever I went. I convinced the owner of the house to give me a lift to the local hospital to get checked out so bad was it, he obliged and took me leaving me there. I was left in a room after explaining my nausea that was by now overpowering me. After around an hour the smell subsided and I got a taxi back to the digs. I later considered the possibility of being drugged but dismissed it. Because of an incident a couple of days later, to this day I am convinced I had somehow been given an insight into what the inside of a death camp smelt like. I do not know how close to the German border I actually was but that was my final summation of the incidents. The next day when we arrived home from work the poor house proud Dutch woman was vigorously scrubbing the floors in the digs. I still owe her an apology, or this explanation. Everything was going fine at work. I was working with a fitter called Mohamed on a stainless steel unit. I was standing at the top of a ladder welding a stainless steel flange when I became aware of small arms fire coming from a clearing nearby, it was quite clear and I questioned Mohamed as to whether there was a firing range nearby, he said "No" I asked him if he could hear the gunfire and he again replied "No" It was loud enough for anyone to hear and took on the sounds of a battle in some sort of clearing close by, I carried on welding and listening to the bemusement of Mohamed, it lasted maybe an hour and then subsided, I said nothing more about it, was it a battle gone by?.

We used to get showered on arrival home thought this particular night I was late and had a long soak in the shower singing, I was singing "The long and winding road" by the Beatles for most of it. I came out of the shower into the next room to smiles from some tourists who where staying there for a couple of nights, they had all been listening. I thought nothing of it and went to my room.

The work finished and it was time to travel home, it had not lasted as long as I wanted but it never seemed to in Holland. I travelled home through Schipol airport as usual. We had received letters about the mortgage arrears saying repossession was now imminent, I made a decision to leave the house and move into my birth home in Aintree with Yvonne and the kids at least we would be safe from the streets. We took some things over and moved in. We had been there for maybe two days when David approached me in the hallway and motioned me into the living room with his head, nothing had been said and there where not any problems with the children, I walked into the living room behind him and he turned and reached behind me to close the door, I wondered what was going on and stood there waiting for him to say something, he calmly took up position right in front of me, waited a few seconds, took a deep breath then lunged at me grabbing me with both hands by the throat, I was struggling to breath, all of this was in total silence, I had never retaliated before in my life, but this was life threatening and I had no choice, I raised my right arm out and over his arms and punched him hard in the left side of his head splitting it open just above the eye, he released his grip immediately and staggered back, he was very sick, it didn't stop there he lunged at me again, by now there was a commotion in the living room, the door opened and two children walked in, it didn't disturb him trying to kill me in front of children and trying to kill me he was, we where all over the living room, I was trying to fight him off, I wasn't attacking, he was murderous in his rage, Yvonne came into the room seeing the scene and shouted to stop and he did then left the living room, he really did have serious problems. We decided to leave for the safety of the children and moved back into our soon to be repossessed home. As we left through the kitchen and back door David standing at the sink stated "Watch your back lad" What had I ever done to him?

I managed to gain some more time in Cammell Lairds it was a welcome break from overseas then after a few weeks I was laid off, it was ship repair and as the ship was finished in the dry dock so was the work. It was Holland again and it was becoming a pain, the work never seemed to last longer than weeks and the agencies promised the earth in work time, I was going to give it another go and see if any of the promises came true. I flew over as usual travelling through Amsterdam, I got on a train and travelled to the digs, I can not remember the name of the place but the road was called Bouven Boukel, it was a very small hamlet and when I arrived I was welcomed in by a nice Dutch lady, her son Ono was there and I got the impression there was no other man at the house, I think she was divorced. I went straight to bed after the usual formalities. Work was not due to start for two days. I got up the next morning and basically sat around watching T.V. Around lunchtime another welder arrived at the back door curiously enough. He was let in by the Dutch lady and she introduced him to me as George Tierney, how she knew him I do not know maybe she just knew his name from the booking, he was from Liverpool as well. He also had a car so travelling to work would be easier. I hardly had any money, so getting to work and getting paid was very important. It was night time when I arrived so I could not see much of the surrounding area, daylight revealed a very isolated area incorporating a lot of farmland and fields. We worked the next couple of days without incident at the factory a few miles away, then the weekend came and their was no work for us, it was a let down, it meant sitting in the digs all weekend with nothing to do and not earning any money. I got the impression that George was on edge and playing some sort of game with me, he was very political. Ono was in the house over the weekend, he was a good bloke, fairly quiet and obviously Dutch. Not knowing each other was a problem George informed me he was a

Catholic, I said I wasn't. Whether he knew who I was I am unaware, though I got the impression he did, he became very overpowering and political, telling me to "Shine" The Saturday passed off without incident the Sunday was going to be another boring day in the digs. After a few hours of sitting around I got up and walked towards the French windows where George was sitting at a table. Looking out across the open fields and looking up at the clear crystal blue sky I said "I love snow" Around a minute later snow flakes as big as your fist started falling all around. George picked up on it immediately saying "Fuck me it's snowing" He had just witnessed one of the paranormal aspects of who I was, that kind of thing was becoming increasingly "Normal" for me to be involved in, it had freaked him out. He became very "Anti" anti Semite, anti Islam and anti monarchy, it was if he was trying to poke me into fame, he was also highly strung. Some time after this we where all sitting watching a T.V programme in the living room, aside from the T.V it was quiet. He turned to me and stated "I am going to fuck your kids" What was going on in his head I do not know, Ono looked at me bemused and nothing was said, we ignored it. He did not have my address and only knew my name, although it was very disturbing to hear. Later on in the afternoon I lost my temper with him and he ran out of the living room, upstairs and locked himself in his room. We did not see him for the rest of the day. We all had rooms on the same landing and that night whilst lying in bed I heard muffled groans coming from Ono's room, they where not normal sounds you would hear, it was the sound of two people in some sort of struggle, I could not be sure what it was at the time so did nothing, not wanting to barge into anyone's room. The next week at work was very awkward he had some sort of problem, as it was, the work was not what was promised and it finished that week, though we had a phone call promising work at another factory. It didn't materialise and we where finished up, having little money I had to gain a lift from George to the nearest busy town to make my way home through Schipol airport. As soon as we got in the car to drive off he said "If you fuck a Dutchman up the arse he'll kill you" It was then that I realised why I had not seen Ono since that night, had George raped him? That is what he was saying to me. He dropped me off in a town some distance away and we spent the night in a hotel, I got up the next morning and he was just gone. I made my way to the airport by train and flew home.

CHAPTER 6

Management

Pretty soon after I arrived home Sheryl Crow released "Every day is a winding road" At first I thought it nothing more than coincidental to my song in the shower until Oasis released "Wonder wall" with the line "And all around the world the roads are winding" Then I wasn't so sure, I felt fairly sure it was the Catholic's and possibly Elizabeth Windsor's "Unknown forces" Was I being watched? and if so how closely? The answer was yes I certainly had been, but I could not be sure I still was, although given who I was it was likely, I was covertly famous remember and according to them Cesar. I had to do something. I phoned up the Liverpool Echo to place an advert in the job section, it went something like this.

> WANTED
> MANAGERS JOB
> BEEN THERE AND DONE IT
> HAVE LIAISED WITH THE BIG BOYS IN DALLAS
> CAN TALK AND LISTEN
> HAVE NEVER BEEN IN CHARGE OF MEN
> HAVE ALWAYS WORKED WITH THEM AND WILL CONTINUE TO DO SO BECAUSE IT WORKS
> IF I CAN NOT DO IT I KNOW A MAN WHO CAN.

I then placed my home phone number 648 3957

followed by my first name Alan, it was a geographical and historical link to me and my address at that time. It cost around £130 and went straight onto the phone bill. What is deemed management in this country is the monarchy or "The firm" as they known or are described. It basically meant I was a King rather than a Cesar, I knew what "The game" was and whilst I was being isolated in my fame I was still self aware and needed my name and fame or my name linked to my fame, the last line, IF I CAN NOT DO IT I KNOW A MAN WHO CAN, was a reference to Jesus Christ. The advert went to print in the Echo and I then received two phone calls one was a young man simply informing me "You've got some balls you lad" That was basically all he said. I then received another call from a man saying he was a car salesman and that he may have an opening as a salesman, I thanked him and politely turned him down. That was it. The advert went into other free press job papers and went international, certainly European. It was to become George W Bush's Noble cause or the Noble cause he spoke of in various speeches during the Iraq conflict. It was, or is also the "Divine inspiration" in the quatrain to Cesar.

No one said anything to me about it although my wife informed me it had gone European, it was all she said. How much she knew about what was going on I was unaware but I felt I could no longer trust her. Not long after this I got some work in Belfast at the shipyard in Harland and Wolfe I had been given the phone number of a company called Ranstaad whilst I had a couple of weeks work in Lairds in Liverpool, I flew over there and we where staying in Banger a few miles outside Belfast, the troubles where still on and we where told to keep ourselves to ourselves. We did for the most part. The landlady from the digs used to give us a lift into work in the morning, I was staying there with Tony a Liverpool lad and a Catholic. I did not have problem with the Catholic's in any bigotry sense. But to be more precise I did not realise just how big of a problem I was going to have with them. Tony and I teamed up and stayed local for the most part when going out drinking. One particular night as we where discussing where to go I stated we should go a little farther down the road to another pub adding jokingly that they might sing "Danny boy" We arrived at the pub and to our surprise a group of people in the lounge where actually singing it, this kind of thing was becoming normal for me, I would say something and it would come to fruition soon after. One morning whilst travelling to work I asked the landlady if they ever had snow there, I don't know why I asked, just a feeling, she said "No" The next day it snowed. That was the way it was for me and had been for a long time. Tony had become nervous being a Catholic in Belfast and decided to mostly stay in the digs, it did not bother me to much. The locals all seemed nice and friendly enough so I carried on going out. I started drinking at a pub called The Penny Whistle in Bangor just down the road, they had a decent juke box and a pool table at the back. I enjoyed a game of pool and was good at it, there only ever seemed to be three people around it, I went over and put some money down and stood back at the bar to wait for my turn, when it came I was to play John. He introduced himself and we broke off, I won the game playing quite well, it attracted the attention of the two other men there who introduced themselves as Tommy and "Shug" I do not know what religion they where or if they where in any way "Connected" but they seemed to be good enough sorts, I am usually pretty good at guessing as to whether someone is Catholic or Protestant, I would guess they where Protestants. I mostly sat on my own when I went in and played pool as and when my turn arose, I got quite friendly with the three of them over a couple of weeks and one night whilst standing in a doorway having a smoke "Shug" came over to me looking a little nervous and sheepish and said "Do you see things?" I did not reply and just bowed my head avoiding the question. The truthful answer would have been "Yes, but I am not going to discuss it with you" and I didn't, the question was not repeated, but it had showed their hand, they knew who I was in the identity sense, it was a form of questioning recognition, I did not mind but why the pretence at not knowing me?. If I was who I was, surely it was a good thing. Another night I felt as if I was being interviewed, I had gone for a walk alone to another pub and two men approached me and started talking to me, they where nervous at first but relaxed after a while and we went to a couple of other pubs, just before they left to go home one of them turned to me and said "I am glad I met you" Turned to his friend and said "Time for peace" I later summarised that they where Loyalists, whether they where or not I am obviously still unaware. I never saw them again. One thing this wasn't was coincidental, whilst working in the yard one afternoon one of the local welders walked past me and said "Lucky bastard" This was after the "Interview" I do not know if there was anything more sinister afoot before "He met me" But it did prick up my ears to something going on and it wasn't paranoia, another peripheral statement referring to me by someone talking to another person was "He's connected alright" I just looked. What can you do or say? Was someone or some body looking after me in Belfast? I didn't know the answer to that either. I did not feel unsafe or under threat in spite of the "Interview!?".

Tony and I went for a walk one Sunday morning to

get some fresh air, we walked around the harbour wall talking about the troubles amongst other things I commented that we where " Next door neighbours" and it all seemed a bit ridiculous that we could not get on, in my ignorance. Tony agreed and then the conversation turned to music and I commented that I thought Robbie Williams the singer from take that was a good entertainer. That was pretty much the way the conversation went. We walked back to the digs and pretty soon the work at the yard finished, early again and we where on our way home. Not until some time later was I unaware that Elizabeth Windsor's "Unknown forces" had just been at work.

I arrived home to hear Tubthumping on the radio soon after with references to "Oh Danny boy, Danny boy" and "Don't cry for me next door neighbour" Direct references to my conversation, I knew it wasn't paranoia when Robbie Williams released "Let me entertain you" They where gaming me and watching me and as much as telling me in song, how it was being done I do not know. But one thing I was sure of, I was right, it wasn't some sort of paranoid or delusional fantasy it was to direct. I was being crowned by the jesters and gamed. "The unknown forces" I didn't know what to do, it was sinister at best. I also believed it to be Catholic based, but how closely was I being watched? and in what domains of my life? I had suspected my phone was tapped but there was no way of telling, but there was a way of finding out. Observed / monitored action and reaction. I started playing up in my own home to find out. Yes I am this clever in this given scenario. I needed evidence. I restricted it to when I was alone and the house was otherwise empty, if they where telling me I was being watched I was going to give them something to watch and see if it was picked up. On one occasion as perverse as it seems I sniffed a pair of knickers, not as disgusting as what they where involved in and I did it with gusto, there was no reaction to it or mention of it, on another occasion I "Kissed my carving knife" whilst preparing a meal for the family whilst they where out, thinking no more of it and for the most part giving up on it. I then heard Shania Twain's "Come on over" with a reference to "I can't believe you kissed your carving knife" Shania Twain is Canadian, how big was this and how big in their "Organisation" was I?! I was furious and trapped, it meant that my children who I loved dearly where being watched as well. I found it very unnerving and more than disgusting. How where they doing it? It was baffling. Though being done to me and mine it undoubtedly was.

We got another letter from the mortgage lender and Yvonne put our names down on the local housing list and convinced me to let her sign for the property and then managed to secure rented accommodation opposite her sisters over in Liverpool and decided to move out sooner, rather than to late and end up on the street, David, the once caring brother and doting uncle didn't care, I decided to stay until the end though I did spend some time over at the rented house. The marriage was finished. I could not salvage it, not with everything that was going on and with who I was historically, it was obvious they where not going to let go. My heart was tearing for the children, they where moving from a detached house in the country to an inner city terraced house. It couldn't have been easy for them and together with the fact that I was no longer there, heartbreaking for me. They should have had a better life.

CHAPTER 7

Losing my home and family

How much I was going to owe on the property after repossession worried me. We had bought it for £70,000 and it was worth more, but we did not have time to sell, it was on the market for £74,000 or there about, it raised little interest. On repossession it was to be auctioned off, if I was lucky and it sold for at least £70,000 I would break even and not owe anything. A vein glimmer of hope arose when I returned to work in the shipyard in Lairds. If I could get enough money together to pay a lump sum off the mortgage I might have been able to save the house, I phoned up the bank one afternoon from work and asked for a loan over the phone. They agreed to it, I asked the woman on the phone to confirm it three times, the last time she was laughing at my disbelief. She had checked my accounts and everything and then confirmed a yes. I would be able to save the house, I was ecstatic. I went home to an empty house void of furniture that night a happier man. The post always arrived after 8am at the house, the next morning I was up at 7am and getting ready for work, the letterbox moved and a letter landed on the mat. I opened it and it was from the bank, they had refused the loan not stating a reason. I was devastated but did not think it suspicious at the time. Even the earlier time of the letter arriving was unusual to normality.

Another incident took place at the camel Laird shipyard which involved a vision I hadn't even realised I had had until it was too late. One day whilst sitting in the tea room eating a bacon sandwich with the lads, I just said "I see Tosh out of the T.V programme the Bill is dead eh!" Nothing was said in reply. Two days later on the front pages of the tabloid press it was a big headline, I had seen it before it had happened without realising, they, the visions where difficult to catch, I never knew when I was having or had one until the reality of the event.

Some time later the work finished again in Lairds and I was back on the dole, going abroad again was out of the question, the work that was promised never materialised and it always seemed to end up worse than when it started. Not wanting to wait for the inevitable I started using my dole money to by paint and some fittings to dress up the house for sale at auction. I decorated downstairs and painted part of the outside. It didn't look like a reconciliation was on the cards as Yvonne wasn't to keen on me staying over in Liverpool, so contact was now minimal. The final repossession order never seemed to arrive and it was some months of waiting. There was a pub over the road called the Basset Hound, it was summer and after decorating I still had enough money for a couple of pints now and again. A very attractive young woman called Vanessa was working behind the bar, I just used to stand there drinking the odd pint, nursing it and taking my time, I was very attracted to her as I have said she was blond and very attractive having a beautiful way with her. I never spoke to her, what was the point? I had no money and not much of a future. We had reached a silent familiarity, the pub was often empty so she was never really busy and always behind the small bar. Whether or not she knew I had feelings for her I do not know, but I did. One late afternoon another barman was behind the bar with her, I used to speak to him. He was a red hot Manchester United fan. The conversation fell silent and the pub was empty.

Vanessa was cleaning glasses in the sink in front of me when she sang the word "Armadillo" towards me. Did she think or was she referring to me as an Armadillo, curling up into a ball in front of her? I said to the barman "Do you know the symbol on the England football shirts, it's a lion isn't it" he confirmed "Yes" though a little curious. If she had called me an Armadillo I had told her I was a lion. I could have been wrong but do not think I was. Nothing more was said, she didn't know my situation and I didn't elaborate. I left the bar for the night soon after. A couple of days later I was back in there, I was sitting in the lounge after finishing painting. It was early afternoon and the pub was otherwise empty. Two men came in and sat at the table directly next to me, one turned to the other one and said "The lion has the gazelle by the throat" It took a minute or so for it to sink in, when it did I found it quite threatening. This is the kind of thing that was going on, covert and sinister. I had a feeling they where protestants though I could be wrong.

The first floor of the house was finished, decorated and painted. One afternoon there was a knock at the door and I answered, it was someone saying they where from the water board looking for payment, it seemed genuine enough until on leaving he held up a copy of a bible with a gold embossed cross on the back and called himself Mr Hyde (Hide) Maybe it was genuine and he was just a bit strange but at this point I was cautious of many things, it was becoming very sinister and I wasn't imagining it either.

It had to be a short period of time now before the house was repossessed, Yvonne came over to the house to remove the fitted fire place, we got on well enough for me to move back in over in Liverpool for a short period. The house was repossessed and it sold for £70,000 so there was no money owing on it. After a short time living in Liverpool a council house in Leasowe on the Wirral became available and we moved over there. It was a three bedroom semi detached property. After a short period of time including Christmas, without warning she threw me onto the street, it was why she wanted to be the sole signer of the property. I ended up sleeping in the car, it was over. After a few days I managed to book myself into a hostel in Birkenhead.

CHAPTER 8

Miracle

I went down to the housing office and put my name down for a flat. I was told to come back in once a week to check on my account. I went back in the next week and sat in a long queue, when I was eventually called to check my application I was told that my details had gone, they had been wiped. I was back to square one. I filled out the relevant forms again with the girl on the computer and left. The next week I went back in to the same scenario. All of my details had been wiped so I went through then same process again. This happened twice more before I finally went in and lost my temper with them, on my doing so, they filled out and processed my application whilst I sat in front of them. They knew something was wrong I had had my details wiped completely four times. A couple of weeks later a flat became available on the Overchurch estate in Upton Wirral. 157 Royden Road and I went to view it. It was a basic two bedroom flat in a four story block on the top floor, with a kitchen and bathroom. I accepted the offer and moved in shortly after. I had nothing and the grant for the cooker, fridge, bed and clothing cupboards was a welcome surprise. I was still unemployed and it needed decorating. I spent some money on a sander and a few other tools along with some white emulsion and began stripping the walls in the living room to decorate. Things where going o.k although the money was tight being on benefit. I could only afford basic food supplies and paying for electric and gas was a large part. I eventually finished the decorating in the living room after stripping and sanding down the walls. I painted the walls white and the skirting boards cream, it looked a bit "Chapelish" but it was comfortable, even without curtains or carpets. I managed to buy a couple of plants and a long stemmed candle holder that stood on the floor in front of the window that I had wiped a whitewash cleaner over and hadn't wiped off. It gave me some privacy until I could get curtains. I did the same in the two bedrooms, though being on the fourth floor no one could see in anyway. I had the small two seat couch, a table and a chair that where given with the grant and an old radio. That was it, it was that basic. The flats where not very well insulated in the sound sense, but the neighbours seemed quiet enough and for the most part whilst decorating and sanding I was the only noise you could hear until I had finished. Nothing was said.

After a couple of months a ship came in for repair and the work picked up at Lairds and I got another start. I now had to start paying rent on the flat every week as the hosing benefit stopped. It was only fifty something pounds per week so it was easy to pay. I bought a decent television set and picked up an old banger Honda sports car for £100. It was a runner, taxed and an M.O.T for twelve months. The money was quite good at Lairds, but it never seemed to last. The ship was finished and soon left, and I was back on the dole. I had become friendly with a good man called Terry from the shipyard and used to go out for a drink with him now and again, it was a welcome break I needed the company. Still not having said anything to anyone surrounding who I was, or what was going on I had for the most part dismissed it, even as serious and perverse as it was. It is the way it gets you. There is no justice for it and very little proof, so why worry? I actually thought they had let me go. I was soon to find out how wrong I was. The paranormal events where about to come into play again as well, one night whilst asleep in the foetal position, I used to sleep that way because it got fairly cold in the bedroom. Whilst asleep I felt someone or something grab a handful of my hair and physically yank my head back as if to cut my throat, my neck audibly cracked backwards as it woke me up. On another occasion whilst asleep again, I became aware of two hands holding me around the ankles and dragging me down the bed, it stopped as I woke up fully, these where becoming regular events. I had bought a church candle to place on the candle holder in the living room and used to sit by candle light at night time watching television. On most nights before I went to bed I had started saying a prayer before it, then blowing it out I would go to bed.

The man in the flat below me had moved out due to rent arrears and a young couple with a small child moved in. Everything was fine at first until late one Friday night they had a blazing row that lasted for hours, they had been out drinking until late, cocaine was mentioned, I could not help but hear it and felt so sorry for the little girl who was their daughter. I did not hear a peep out of her. It was to become a regular occurrence until it became very sinister with my unwanted involvement, he was a sick man.

Money was tight and the benefit I was receiving only lasted for twelve days out of the fourteen it was supposed to. To fill in the gaps for food I used to walk down to the beach and get cockles and muscles in a bucket to eat during the monetary shortfall. It played a part. I missed the children terribly and did not have much contact with them if any at all, Marybeth had been to the flat once and she had had a bath. They did not live far away but the relationship with Yvonne was such that no or little contact was best. I then received a letter through the post from the housing office stating that I owed them over £500 for rent arrears, I didn't, my rent was fully paid up as and when I was working, I paid it religiously and when I wasn't working the housing benefit took over as I claimed for it, I was furious and ignored the letter to my detriment. Someone was playing games and I wasn't imagining it. The arguments in the flat below where now regular and Robbie, the male, had taken to audibly raping his girlfriend, without a care who was listening or could overhear, it went on for months and everyone in the flats must have known so loud was it. Not having any work I decided to do something for my children by way of an explanation for them. I would write them the story of who I was. I got some A4 sheets of paper and began writing a story not dissimilar to this. I got to the part in the story where Vanessa the bar maid called me an Armadillo and finished for the night. I got up the next morning and switched on the television to see an Armadillo across the bottom of the screen on the I.T.V or BBC news channel, yes I know how ridiculous that sounds, but you have to remember who I am, it was for no apparent reason and it wasn't linked to anything or mentioned, it was just there in cartoon form. I, like you, dismissed it. I was big enough to warrant that kind of attention and perversion but was I being watched in the flat? I knew Diana Spencer was sane by definition of knowledge and the evidence I had, even if I could not prove it I knew. They want you to know, but only you in isolation. Such alone can prophecy, referring to the quatrain to Cesar. The attacks on the world trade centre had just happened and all hell was about to break loose. I like many other people found it very disturbing.

The arguments and turmoil in the flat below where now a regular occurrence, it was every Friday night and Robbie was a wife beating rapist bully. He was smaller than me and I am only five foot six inches, his girlfriend was smaller than him. The little girl must have been no more than two years of age. He had a serious problem. This particular Friday night I was dreading it, just sitting there in the flat waiting. I had a couple of pounds to spare this particular Friday so decided to go out for a couple of pints. I arrived back around 11o'clock and waited for it, part way drunk I decided to pre-empt it, I picked up a sledge hammer I had from the shipyard and began throwing it around the flat, allowing it to fall heavily on the floor, loudly whooping and shouting "YEE HAA!" It went on for around ten minutes and then I stopped and shouted "Did you get the message?" No reply came and the flats fell silent. They all must have known why I had done it. A few minutes later there was a knock on my door, I opened it to a police officer and said "What?" he told me there had been a noise complaint, I asked him to come in and in a loud voice explained exactly what was going on stating it was every Friday night and then some further stating loudly that "I have never heard that poor kid laugh" The police officer said no more and left. He understood.

I wasn't expecting a reaction to the action and I thought no more of it until a few days later Bruce Willis appeared on a chat show brandishing a sledge hammer smashing up a pile of C.D's to great applause and laughter from the audience. Still in denial of the possibility I was being full on watched, I then watched an American General on a news report take to the stage to give a speech with a sledgehammer over his shoulder saying "It is hammer time!" before going into Iraq. It wasn't paranoia, I was being watched in my own home it was only confirmed to me when another news report on Belfast revealed a statement painted on a corrugated iron fence "Under New Management" I was being used, they knew I was a King or a Protestant leader, I had the jesters and the entertainment industry watching me and I was being gamed or used as a leader, possibly by the loyalists. It was disgusting, my daughter had had a bath in that flat and that was the kind of people involved in it, they where not even English and this was in Britain. I was a world leader admittedly but this was beyond the pale. I didn't mind being used as one because of who I was but this was very sinister, I wasn't imagining it either. Sarah Ferguson had told Diana Spencer to lift up the floorboards to check for bugs and or cameras, I had not checked out the flat or the house at 116 Barnston Road that was repossessed but nothing was visible to the open or naked eye. I had no idea how it was being done. I racked my brains as to what to do about it, there was very little so big was it.

Robbie in the flat below had obviously been told who I was by someone and at first obviously didn't care. The arguments and the rape in the flat below continued and on one of the Friday nights he was actually shouting off the balcony to someone that "It means he'd stab you" He was referring to the quatrain to Cesar, me as they thought, there is part of it where it states "The knives are out for you now Cesar" that is the way it was, everyone knew of the advert in the Liverpool Echo I had placed and who I was. What they did not know was the truth surrounding what was actually being done to me in the privacy of my own home and the perversion my children had been party to. He was very sick and after one seriously evil night of rape. The next morning he was crying like a child with snot coming out of his nose saying "I am dead, I am dead" He was then on the phone to someone stating that he had been possessed the night before, it was very sick and evil. The people watching me must also have heard all that was going on in the flat below. Everyone in the flats knew about it and him. I had heard him verbally abusing his daughter as well, something that had upset me as I love children.

I was getting tired, mentally as well as physically, it was all getting on top of me, my back was playing up from the fall on the rig, it kicked off every eighteen months or so and became quite debilitating. I could feel it coming on, I got warning spasms before it seized completely. It usually lasted around five days and then subsided. I was trying to catch it before it did fully seize. I started having hot baths and soaking in the water until the water cooled. This particular day I had already had two hot baths. I really was mentally tired. My prayers had been getting answered and together with the monitoring it really was getting to me. I ran the third bath of the day, it was early evening and I took the candle into the bathroom with me and left the lights off. I got in the bath and rather than lie back I curled into a small ball resting my head on my forearms which where in turn resting on my knees. I let my mind go blank and just sat there. The water cooled after some time and I got out of the bath. I blew out the candle and turned on the light. It was then that I noticed a magnetic black ring around the water line of the bath. It was around an inch and a half thick and went around the full bath. The bath was spotless beforehand and I was physically clean. I had been washed in the bath. "Come to me all of those who are weak and weary and I will give you rest" There was no other explanation to cause the reaction, it was mystifying and undeniably something out of the ordinary. I took it in my stride. I also felt better.

Watching a live show with Tony Blair appearing on it sometime after this I stood in my own living room and called him a "Lying Bastard" He sat back in his chair as if he had been gut shot. Little did I know that they where soon to be exposed with a miracle. Whether that incident with Blair was a coincidence or not, this was exposure of the voyeurs. Some further time later it was a Wednesday afternoon and I had a headache coming on, it came on quite quickly and pretty soon I was in agony, I had no money for pain killers and it was getting really serious, so bad was the pain I was cradling my head in my forearms and kneeling down with my forehead resting on the bed. I could not get comfortable so bad was the pain. I had had a migraine once as a child and this was far worse. It lasted for twenty four hours and then passed. The relief was immense, I had not been watching T.V all of the way through it and spent the Friday in bed so had not seen any news. I got up on the Saturday morning and switched on the T.V to see a T.V programme called C.D.U.K. It was a music programme airing live on a Saturday morning presented by a woman called Cat Deeley and two co presenters called Ant and Dec. I sat and watched for a few minutes. Then it was announced that George Harrison had died on the Thursday and they where going to play a tribute song for him called "My sweet Lord" Jesus Christ? Around five foot five or six, dark collar length hair, more than a growth less than a beard, dark middle eastern skin tone, portly more than athletic, wears a white smock, not a robe, with a straw rope belt tied around the waist, with the tassel's finishing at the right knee with two knots at the ends, outstretched arms and upturned palms with a warm welcoming smile. I was sitting down at the time. Yes, I know how unbelievable it is, I saw him in Bouven Boukel in Holland. One day it will come out true. I am this big and they damn well know it. I was devastated at his death, it was a real shock. There had been nothing on the news about any illness and then he was just dead. Maybe it was my family links to Brian Epstein or the Beatles, but I, possibly like so many other people felt close to them. The tribute song started and I began to weep, I filled the whole room with a white light it lasted for the song and then cut back to the studio audience when it finished. Ant and Dec and Cat Deeley where crying, either Ant or Dec looked straight into the camera and said "Are you doing this?" Emma Bunton was running around the studio as if in a puddle of wee saying "We are going to stop "The game" We are going to stop the game" Cat Deeley then said something to redress the "Problem" They had been caught, how it was being done I still do not know, but the archive footage of the live T.V programme is still available to view, as I have said it aired live on I.T.V two days after George Harrison's death on the Saturday. I had just passed George Harrison to God. Believe it or not, that is the truth of it and surrounding it. Elizabeth Windsor went to see the Pontiff with an oil painting soon after. It was the Catholic's and they had just inadvertently exposed themselves, VISIBLY. They were doing to me what was being done to Diana Spencer. Unlike her, I had no voice of objection in any domain. Who could I turn to or tell? I felt very uncomfortable in the flat and went out soon after for some peace and solace, I had just worked a miracle, I walked into a nearby pub and ordered a glass of coke and a young man came up to me with tears in his eyes looked straight at me and called me "A lying bastard" I believe Catholic. So what did the miracle mean in real terms? Well, it meant I was a True King, you see, miracles translate to truth and truth translates to justice, justice in the British domain is nobility and judgement. It also meant I now had a licence to kill given who I was together with the power and miraculous ability in truth and judgement, a licence of defence. It also meant I was the Head of The Protestant Faith by miraculous deed and definition, the whole nine yards. It was that, that was being stolen from me and mine. I loved "Mine" my children where lovely and caring, I used to take them out whenever the opportunity arose. One one particular occasion it was conquer season and they where full on the trees. There was a very old conquer tree in a church yard just along Barnston Road around a mile from where we lived, they had been asking me to take them to collect conquers. This particular day I had time and said "Come on then" They asked if Robert and Liam could come along, their friends from around the corner and I said "Yes" We walked the short distance to the churchyard and entered, it was deserted. The kids ran towards the tree and I looked for a stick or branch to throw into the tree to get them to fall, it was going to be difficult as the tree was overhanging the main road and I was worried about the stick landing on a passing car. Then Liam shouted over to me "Is it o.k if we walk on the graves Alan" I said "No they wont mind us being here as long as we don't walk on the graves" With that, just about every conquer on the tree fell to the ground in one fell swoop, it was amazing. They where everywhere and the melee that followed was hilarious, the kids where diving everywhere for them, Just another not so normal event in my life.

Time passed in a now unacceptable situation and I was soon to find out how much of an invasion Robbie from the flat below was to become in my life. I needed money for the children, work was still sporadic and at this point I was unemployed. My solicitor was called Fanshaw Porter and Hazlehurst, they where based in Birkenhead. I used the miracle the only way I could, I needed the house sold and quickly to give my children some money and some sort of a future with me in it. I started to write a document to my solicitor surrounding the house of my birth and my inheritance. I did not finish it in the flat feeling to uncomfortable there. So I took what I had written and jumped on the bus and went down to the solicitors in Rock Ferry Wirral, I stopped at a pub just around the corner to finish it off, I basically explained who I was and that I needed the house sold and suggested just selling my share on the back of my fame, I also explained why I was being watched as well, I finished it in the pub and then took it around the corner to the solicitors and hand delivered it, it was accepted at the front desk and put into a pigeon hole. I got on the bus to go home and was confronted by two men who stated "It's the midnight mass I can't handle" Was it in reference to my nightly prayers?

Sitting in my flat the next afternoon, I heard that document being read out loud in the flat below me with the question to a woman by Robbie "Where did he write this?" The reply was, "He wrote it in a pub in Rock Ferry" A solicitor of the bar had handed out the document to someone, a total stranger to me. Later on that night he had made the equation or worked out that if I was being watched, he was being listened to, he then repeated the "I am dead" sob. What the hell was going on, this was my solicitor, a solicitor of the bar in Great Britain allowing or handing out a document from a personal client to nothing more than a rapist or wife beating drug dealer and no, to repeat and re-state, I was not imagining this either, they where up to no good, miracles where not far away now and I knew it. I was very annoyed and dealing with extreme power, the ultimate power. My prayers really where being answered and it wasn't a game, I was being destroyed. On some nights I used to sit in silence with just a candlelight burning and the T.V switched off before prayer, on this occasion I was staring into space and out of the window, I just said "Give them an earthquake" The very next day an earthquake shook the country on a magnitude not seen before. That is the kind of power I was dealing with, I was harnessing or starting to harness the paranormal.

A pub called the Overchurch was a couple of hundred yards away along the road, I used to have a couple of pints and a game of pool in there every now and again, it had a small bar with a pool table and a T.V over the doorway around seven foot off the floor, the lounge was in the back. There where around eight people in there that made the small bar look quite full, it was quiet and the jukebox was off. I was playing pool with one of the locals, whilst waiting for him to take his shot I turned away from the table and started to watch the T.V over the door. Who wants to be a millionaire was on and the woman had just won the million pounds. It was then that my opponent approached me and asked me what I was watching, I told him I had just been watching some woman win the million on "Who wants to be a millionaire" adding that the picture wasn't very good and he went quiet, I took my shot and turned again to watch the T.V and noticed it had not even been plugged in, four of the people who where sitting watching the pool got up and left, I had been watching a blank T.V screen according to them. According to me I had been watching a T.V programme and I was, the next week I watched the same woman win on the same programme whilst sitting in my flat, I had a witnessed vision, one I could not deny. I had seen a week into the future. As strange and enlightening as it was there was nothing I could do it was just part of who I was. Had it not been for noticing the T.V wasn't even plugged in I would not have known that I had just had a vision and been oblivious to it. I also enjoyed cooking and was quite good at it, deboning and sauces etc, I had bought a duck and some vegetables with potatoes. I deboned the duck and stuffed it with garlic and vegetables and boiled the bones and excess meat and made a sauce. I cooked and eat it, it was nice and after sitting on the chair for an hour decided to go for a pint. I was standing at the bar having a pint on my own when a man walked in and stood beside me and ordered a pint and said to the group of men next to him "The duck looked nice didn't it lads" I said nothing, there is nothing you can say for accusations of madness or paranoia. No way was it coincidental. I was being watched, but how the hell where they doing it?

I had gained employment again, Terry had given me a phone number for a company called Arnway, they did repair work on cement making furnaces globally and the money was good, with accommodation thrown in, it was a welcome break from the flat and situation. I did a trip and gained some money, it was job and finish. I held some of the money back, I had decided on something to do. I would go and speak to someone about it, far enough away so as not to be followed. I had just enough money to book a coach to Berlin. I packed a bag and put some cheap cans of tuna in it with a knife to open them. It was this serious, I boarded the coach and set off for Berlin, on arrival I located the British Consulate and thinking it was both secure enough and far enough away I went in to address the issues I had surrounding the illegal and perverse surveillance along with the concerns for my children. I walked into the Consulate and was met by Ken DeRoche' a Consulate official who was behind a bullet proof glass screen, I started to explain to him why I had come to Berlin and he listened for a few minutes, I explained to him about the phones being tapped along with the other monitoring and how serious I thought it was, he asked for my passport and took it away with him and punched some details into a computer across the room. He then turned and made his way back to the counter and almost laughed in my face as he handed me back my passport. I was then dismissed. I left the Consulate in disbelief. It was serious to warrant a sit down conversation at least. People where being watched in their own homes and it involved foreign nationals, surely it was a national security concern!? I had evidence! I hitch hiked back to Britain, it took two days and travelling without food or water by this time. I got home hungry and disillusioned at the arrogance of my own country. I was now totally at a loss as to what to do, it was not something I could ignore either, I wasn't being allowed to ignore them, a whole host of records came out with possible links to me and who I was. David Grey Babylon, Robbie Williams Something beautiful (You can't manufacture a miracle) and "We've been expecting you" Oasis "The Hindu Times" with the line "God gave me some of your rock 'N' roll brain". Again, I wasn't imagining this either, it all made sense to me what they, "They" being the jesters where doing, in Emma Bunton's "Game" The same "Voyeuristic Prophecy Game" that T'Pau are singing about. I had tried to tell the truth to them and they would not listen, maybe Ken DeRoche' already knew I was telling the truth I do not know. Still, no one had given me any recognition apart from covert "In your ear" information. I was lost in the game, with an incredible amount of power. I then received another red letter from the housing office saying they where taking court action, it was money I did not owe. I was being stitched up and forced onto the street, but why? Did I know too much? How could anyone be so stupid? This was amazing. They had their wildest dreams locked up, miracles, prophecy and the possibility of a lasting peace and they where doing this, it was madness. They gave me a court date to appear for a repossession hearing on the flat. I had nothing to lose, I wrote a scathing letter to the court and told them who I was and what was going on, i.e I was being watched and having my details wiped from computers. I told them I was not going to bother appearing. It was basically contempt of court, it was at this point contempt I had for them. The court date came and passed and then I received a letter stating that I could pay off the arrears at £2 per week, what was said in court I am unaware. It didn't help the situation much I was still in the same position. At a loss I decided to phone up the newspapers, I tried the Daily Mail and told them I was being watched in my own home and that my phones where being tapped, I then explained that I had worked a miracle. I had a story basically, the man on the phone said he wasn't interested. I then tried three other newspapers, one was the Daily Mirror, I got the same results from the other three, they where not interested. Taking issue and having been quoted by politicians I then decided to phone up the political parties and address my concerns, I first tried the Labour party and the man who answered stated "If we where tapping your phones we would not admit it would we?!" A curious statement, I then in turn tried the Conservatives and told them I had a serious issue and problem, they just about laughed in my face. That was the attitude of them. "Unlucky mate" Thinking the only option I had was to leave. I then got a phone call one night. It was 4a.m in the morning and on answering a disguised voice on the other end of the phone stated "I have found a very expensive piece of jewellery lad, it's a watch, I found it in a cosy" It sounded very much like David with his voice disguised. It was disguised with a very broad, guttural Liverpool accent. I put the phone down and it immediately rang again with the same statement, it was very threatening. So what did it mean, well it actually gave me some information. It was in reference to the game. The part where he states "I have found a very expensive piece of jewellery" is a reference to being Jewish. He had found a Jew."It's a watch" was in reference to watching basically, he was watching a Jew and he was also informing me he knew who I was, the reference to "Cozy" was in reference to a Ford Cosworth car, I think it was a car David was driving around in at the time. He was telling me I was being watched basically, something I obviously already knew, but more than that he was telling me it was him that was watching me. It wasn't, it was an awful lot bigger he just wanted to instill a threat in his sickness. That is the kind of coward he was. I had to get out of there, it was inhumane and evil. If you have a conversation with someone and offer an opinion that is used in any domain of life, that is one thing and fair enough, but having your phones tapped and being watched in the privacy of your living room along with your loved ones is a completely different matter.

I got another spell at Cammell Lairds on nights and decided I had no alternative other than to leave to gain some sort of a life. I saved up some money from the work and made plans to leave. I moved the cooker and other stuff out of the flat and onto the landing outside and then I knocked at the girls flat across the landing. I told her that the stuff was hers and that she should sell it for what she could get for it and take the kids out with the money. I wasn't coming back. I then packed some clothes and went to the airport and booked a flight to Tel Aviv in Israel, I was going for political asylum. I did not know what else to do or where else to go. I travelled through Frankfurt and arrived in Tel Aviv. I was going to start a new life and had not told anyone, I had not even informed the kids. Which grieved me deeply, I missed them so much. On arrival I queued up to go through the customs, there was all kinds going through my head, what was I going to say to them at the border control? "I want political asylum" "I am on holiday" to try and get through, "I have worked miracles, am being persecuted and come to the Holy land for a new life!" I elected on telling the truth, it seemed to be the best policy. I walked up to the desk as my turn arose and simply handed the woman my passport and said "I would like political asylum" She looked at me for a minute and then took my passport away and returned a few minutes later with two security staff, I explained as best I could in the short time I had, the complex situation I was in, inclusive of miracles and the Windsor aspect of my being. i.e The threat I was to them just being alive and working miracles. I did not actually state that I was a King. I was marched out like the original "Nutter" and put in a holding tank, I was told that basically because I was from Britain there was no asylum required because of the human rights legislation the country had or was supposed to have. It was basically "You don't need it" They didn't believe me anyway. I was kept in a holding tank for 24hrs and as they where marching me out I was told never to return to Israel again. I was then put on a plane and flown back to Great Britain.

On my arrival back at the flat I had nothing, Just a bed and some furniture, No cooker or T.V and I was still in the same situation. I had no money and no means of cooking food. It was back down to picking shellfish off the beach at Morton shore. I had bought some small camping candles to cook with. I put the cockles and muscles into a stainless steel bowl and cooked them over the candle flame in some water. That is how I eat for some time until my state benefit came through, when it did I decided I was not going to stay in the flat, I was being driven out anyway. I decided on some respite and bought a cheap two man tent, I had been speaking to an Aunt who lived local and she told me about a retreat in Scotland where you could just go to and stay, it was called Sami Lyng's. It was some sort of Buddhist retreat. I went down to the coach station and booked a ticket to Scotland. I bought the now usual tins of tuna fish to eat on my journey and whilst I was there. I boarded the coach and set off for Scotland. I arrived and just pitched a tent on some land on the property, nothing was said and no one bothered me. There where other people their who where milling around on the "Holy site" but for the most part we all kept ourselves to ourselves I used to go for soup in the dining hall of an afternoon, the rest of the time I spent sitting alone by the river on a bench. After around a week my own tinned food had nearly ran out so I started making plans to leave, I did actually feel better I had enjoyed the break. Whilst there I was thinking about what I was to do and I decided to return to Aintree and broach the subject of living in a house I part owned with David who I suspected was not even living there. I packed up my things and wrote a sign ready to hitch hike back to Liverpool, I didn't even have enough money to get home. After a long day and nights hike and hitch I arrived back in Liverpool in the early afternoon. I called into a friends who lived local to the Old Roan and had a cup of tea and something to eat. His wife was home alone and I didn't discuss anything surrounding the conspiracy. We had a chat for around an hour and as I was leaving, she kindly gave me a twenty pound note. It was nice, we had been childhood friends. I decided to walk the mile or so to my old house in Aintree. When I got there I knocked on the door and there was no answer. Not knowing what to do and unsure as to whether David was even living at the property, the gardens where overgrown and the house looked quite bad in the upkeep sense. I decided to walk around to a friends house to get something to force entry, I was part owner of the property remember and David had changed all of the locks on the house. I borrowed a hammer and a wood chisel, I then walked back around to the house and began to carefully take the putty out of one of the side windows on the house, as I was doing so Mrs Riddock, one of the neighbours from across the road came over and asked me what was going on with the house, I said she knew more than me and she then informed me that no one had seen David for some time and asked if everything was alright, I assured her it was and that I just didn't have any keys and was unaware of David's whereabouts. She left and I finished removing the window. I placed it in the back garden safely planning to replace it as soon as I could. I climbed through the window into the house. It hadn't been lived in, the lights where blown or removed and all of his fishing gear was in the living room. There really was something going on and there really was something wrong with him. No body could be this cruel to a member of their own family and especially the children, my children. He didn't even want the house to live in. Yet was it fear of the paranormal events in the house? That was probably part of it. He was a coward. I phoned up a solicitor to confirm I was within my rights breaking in as a part owner and he confirmed that I was. I then went upstairs and the lights where out there as well, I then walked into the small front bedroom and lay on the bed, remembering the time Jack and I had slept there not long after my mother's death. I had been awoken to a hooded and cloaked figure standing over me in the bedroom and I cried out in shock waking Jack up and he started crying. I was about to realise in events to follow soon that it was Michelle Nostradamus the writer of the quatrain to Cesar. It began to get dark when I heard a car pull up outside so I got up and looked out of the window to see who it was. It was David, he had closed the car door and looked up and immediately noticed the missing window pane, I opened the bedroom window and shouted out to him that it was only me and there was nothing to worry about. I then closed the window and made my way to the top of the stairs, by which time David was already in the hallway, he looked up at me at the top of the stairs and before I could say anything he said "I am going to kill you" He then walked straight into the kitchen and removed a ten inch carving knife from the knife block and walked back into the hall and then began to run up the stairs brandishing it, he was serious, he was this sick and always had been, he had serious problems. I retreated into the small bedroom having nothing to defend myself with and closed the door. He was at the door in an instant I could hear him grunting and puffing in his rage as he tried to force the door handle down that I was holding to gain entry and stab me, he was psychotic and it was only me who had ever seen this side of him as the abuse. I knew he was capable of it and as I held my phone in my free hand I said I was phoning the police, he said he loved them and he was going to kill them as well, the door began to bulge with his full weight against it. After around ten minutes of ranting rage and mutterings the door panel went back to it's normal shape, I released my grip on the door handle and gently opened the door, he had retreated and was standing in the bathroom doorway with the ten inch carving knife in his hand. I tried to talk to him to no avail, he was grunting and talking incoherently. I managed to get him to listen and told him I was going to leave, he had serious psychological problems. I had suffered over thirty years of murderous abuse from him and knew him well and he was smaller than me, he was very devious miserly and sly, he always had been. I edged my way towards the top of the stairs and walked down them, he was right behind me with the carving knife and then followed me out into the street with it. Then having some room to manoeuvre in the street I addressed the situation with him and told him he was going down for this (Prison) He was still brandishing the carving knife in the middle of the street. I then again walked around to my friend Willie's. I explained to him what had just happened and he told me to phone the police which I did, I explained to them what had just happened and they said they would send a car around to the house. I walked back around to the house and just as I arrived the police car pulled up with one officer in it. I motioned to him and walked over to the car and I got in, I again explained the situation and that he had a carving knife. The officer was reluctant to knock at the house and decided to drive me up to the police station at Copy Lane. On our arrival I was taken in to an interview room and to my surprise was informed that David had just arrived. I found out later or to be more precise I worked out that after I had left the house he had followed me around to willies without me knowing. For what reason I am unaware, maybe he was looking for a quiet place to deal with or kill me. It was then that another police officer came into the interview room and rounded on me saying David was in the other room crying, he was this devious, sly and sick. The officer had obviously been taken in by David's tears and woeful innocence. I, as the abused was dumbstruck. He had just attempted a murder, not for the first time and then burst into tears in front of the police and got away with it!? It was some time after this that I realised what the quatrain to Cesar meant when it made reference to "The knives are out for you now Cesar" It meant that after over 30yrs of abuse he had finally resorted to pulling a knife on me to try to kill me. As unbelievable as you may find that information, it is true, I have lived that quatrain. I was then told by the police to stay away from the house, my own home that I had rights to. I had no alternative other than to return to the flat.

The situation was horrendous. I had to get out of there. After another week or so of living off the beach until my social payment arrived, I decided to go out for a drink, I went into Birkenhead in the afternoon and walked around a couple of pubs. I wasn't drunk but had enough to be feeling down, where could I turn for justice? As who I was, I could not approach the police as they where adhering to a different house, the house of Windsor, they did not have the evidence and again as who I was I outranked her and them by way of miraculous definition, they where not the Heads of State in my company, BUT, I had no choice I had to offer them the evidence of the conspiracy, I was alone and had been put on my own. All of the loyalists had connections to the monarchy in pretence, the Windsor's, the rest of the Protestants where in ignorance and I had not written any evidence down apart from the story I was writing, but I had stopped writing that and it was incomplete. I stupidly thought that they would believe me. That they would take my word for it, it was true, why wouldn't they? You have to remember how covertly famous I had been made. I was being watched, I was being gamed and used. It was a conspiracy they had to be made aware of in light of Diana Spencer and others! I decided I had no choice and walked into Hamilton Square police station and approached the front desk. I said to the officer behind the desk that I had a problem I needed dealing with, I was being watched in my own home and my phones where being tapped along with having my details altered or removed from computer databases. He asked me to repeat it and I did, he asked me to wait a minute and walked away from the desk, on his return he motioned me through a side door and into an interview room, he said "We are going to help you Alan" I was relieved, at last some form of redress. I sat in the interview room and waited for around ten minutes and then the door opened and three people with overcoats on walked in and sat down in chairs opposite to me. They introduced themselves as psychiatrists. The police had got straight on the phone to the mental health. I sat and explained the situation to them and told them I was being gamed and watched basically, they listened and smiled at all the right moments. Then they said they again, "Where going to help me!" they had asked for a number of a next of kin and I had given my aunts number to them. Then after around half an hour of my explanation, they got up and again said they where going to help me and led me through to the front desk again, I was then confronted by my aunt and uncle who where standing there. They said it was going to be alright and smiled, I was then led out to a waiting ambulance outside the police station. I got in without complaint although I was devastated, this was horrendous, I was telling the truth and it wasn't a "Psychiatric" truth. I then decided on silence as being the best policy, as I have said although I had started to write the story I had not finished it and didn't have the literal evidence to produce, I had foolishly thought the police where police and my word would be enough to warrant some form of an enquiry. The ambulance drove to Clatterbridge mental health unit and I was led in, I later found out I had been what is called "Sectioned" under the mental health act. It was new to me as I had never heard it before. I was then informed that I was to have a hearing in the morning to discuss the state of my mental health. I was seriously worried all of this had stemmed from going into the police station with a legitimate complaint. My aunt and uncle went home saying they would be back the next morning at the relevant time to attend the hearing. I was then led to the Kensington ward where I was to spend the night, I understandably didn't get much sleep and got up the next morning and waited around until the hearing. At the relevant time my aunt turned up and walked in, we waited outside the room for them to prepare for us and then after a few minutes we where called in. We where faced with a panel of people and I was told that I could not, or was not allowed to speak until spoken to. Present at the meeting was Sir Ronald and the rest of the panel where made up of Pakistani in origin people. One woman, a Pakistani psychiatrist called Dr Parhee was in charge of the meeting and Sir Ronald was to oversee it, there was a woman of English origin taking notes and three Pakistani underlings to Dr Parhee. Sitting opposite all of this was me and my aunt. I had obviously at this point realised I had gone to the wrong "Windsor" house to tell the truth. They had a conversation around me, I was asked if I understood why I was there and I confirmed that I was. I wasn't really included in the meeting until Dr Parhee asked me if I thought I was being watched, I said "I believe we are all being watched over, but yes I believe I am being mortally watched as well" I then in slight anger at the stitch up that was going on asked her what she believed in and what her belief structure involved as I believed in miracles and miraculous events knowing hers involved a woman with eight arms. With that my fate was sealed. All of the while I was glancing over at Sir Ronald who spent the entire meeting sitting their making sure his powder blue handkerchief in his suit top pocket was geometrically square with the rest of his suit and rearranging his matching powder blue tie unable to look me in the eye. I wasn't diagnosed with anything to my face at that point but after a break in proceedings and waiting outside the room again with my aunt, they came out a few minutes later and informed me I had been sectioned and was to spend some time on the ward for "Treatment" I decided there and then that I would speak no more. The next day I contacted a solicitor and explained the situation and that i had been sectioned after working a miracle, I briefly explained the situation to him and he said to contact him the next day. Dr Parhee then came onto the ward. I got the impression or found her to be a nasty authoritarian. Little did I know at that time but she was later to falsify medical records and drug administration charts of mine. I was called into a room with her and some students she was trying to impress. I elected on silence and just sat there, educating them and her was impossible, she told me she wanted me to take some drugs, I declined saying I would not take drugs of any kind from her, she repeated the request a couple more times again to my refusal, given I wasn't forthcoming with conversation, the meeting ended and I walked back to my room. Soon after a lovely Irish nurse called Briege came into my room and sat on the edge of the bed and tried to convince me to take the drugs I was being told to take, I refused saying that I wasn't mentally ill and explained to her how I had worked a miracle and caught some unsavoury people in some very unscrupulous acts of gross perversion. She then took my hand and tried further to convince me, she was lovely but ignorant to the truth. At that moment Dr Parhee appeared in the doorway of my room with two male members of staff informing me that if I did not agree to taking the drugs she would have me strapped to a bed and forced to take them, I again refused and she left the doorway, I had done nothing to warrant this kind of treatment. Briege then tried to explain to me that she would actually have it done. In other words she was capable of it. I again refused and she left my room. I was then left alone for around a week during which time I had a visit from one of my old and close school friends Dave, he didn't know what to say and I didn't know how to explain to him how famous I actually was. He sat there quietly nervous before his old friend who had gone off the rails a bit. I just said to him, "You have a very famous friend" He gave me a half smile, stayed a little while longer and left. I had been labelled mentally ill. It was the worst possible situation I could have thought of. I could not do this to anyone, I had phoned back the solicitor and told him that I was the man who had phoned earlier and worked the miracle and been sectioned. He then asked me "What miracle?" I put the phone down on him, there was no redress and no justice for it. It was too big, as was I. Another meeting was arranged with Dr Parhee after around a week and again she brought in all of her students. She informed me that I was to be released. I had shown no signs of anything other than normality throughout the entire ordeal. I was moved onto the next ward which wasn't a lock down ward for the night and was released the next day. Having refused and not been given, forced or otherwise, drugs in any way shape or form. No reason was given for the release, though I did inform Dr Parhee before leaving that millions of people knew who I was, she was silent. If you take the numeracy of all of the people who where listening to the music, then that is how famous I was or indeed am and that is an awful lot of people listening to the music in ignorance of my being. "Liverpool, Rotterdam, Rome" alone by Beautiful South introduced me to millions of people, albeit covertly. So I wasn't insane, paranoid or delusional. They just didn't know my name.

I returned to my flat, it was an empty void and I was alone again only this time labelled mentally ill, a bit of a nut case to be felt sorry for or feared. If it got out it wouldn't effect my ability to work, but it probably would effect my ability to gain employment. I didn't say anything to anyone, if they knew, they knew basically. There was nothing I could do about it. The work had picked up again at Lairds in the shipyard and I phoned up looking for work, I was successful and also curious as to how much they knew about my incarceration, again I said nothing of it. The rape and abuse in the flat below continued in spite of what he had read. The whole situation was getting to me. I was going to leave for good, I could not even have my own children around to the flat, something that was also getting to me and I could not even tell them why. I could not without evidence, even tell them who I was. It was heartbreaking for me, I was going to have to leave for good and leave them behind without an explanation. It wasn't fear it was desperation. I saved up some of the wages from Lairds and had over a thousand pounds. I went down to the travel agents and booked a flight to New York costing around £700 I think it was and made arrangements to leave, I say made arrangements but I did not actually tell anyone, I just changed some money to dollars. On the day of the flight I packed a bag with some clothes in, everything basically, I stored my welding certificates in a safe place in the bag in case I managed to gain employment, they where valid the world over. I made my way to Manchester airport and waited for my flight to New York. When the time arrived I could not bring myself to get on the flight, something didn't feel right, something was wrong and I didn't know what it was, I let the flight time pass and didn't get on the flight, I returned to the flat and lost all of the money for the flight.

CHAPTER 9

New York

March 1st 2004

The work in Cammell Lairds was still on and I regained employment there for a few weeks. Still intent on having to leave I saved up some more money again, re booked my flight to New York and changed the very little money I had left into dollars. This time I was going to leave, I had no choice, if I was going to gain any form of a life and freedom I had to leave everything behind. The day before I went I went around to the Leasowe estate to say goodbye to the children, when I arrived they where all playing out in the street and Marybeth and Emily had seen me walking up and ran over. I was heartbroken but didn't let it show, I was going to miss them growing up, Emily was only five and to try to explain to them both who I was and what was going on would be impossible. They ran up to me and I said "Hi" I did not know how to begin so I just blurted it out that I was going to be leaving tomorrow for America and I loved them very much. Emily was more interested in showing me how brave she was holding a worm in the palm of her hand and didn't fully understand, Marybeth was more aware and I took her head between both of my hands, holding either side of her head and looking her straight in the eyes I said "If you want to contact me, or try to get in touch with me for anything, get in touch with the White House in America and tell them who you are" She was speechless and said "O.k" I was George Bush's Noble cause remember and NO, I wasn't imagining it, how do you tell a child that you are being used by the organisation to run it. I glanced over to the small grass field outside the house and saw Jack smiling and laughing playing rounder's with the rest of the kids, I couldn't bring myself to go over and say goodbye to him, so I told Marybeth to get him on his own after I had gone and to tell him I loved him very much, I didn't bother knocking at the house to see Yvonne and just left. I left everything behind and didn't know what was to become of me, I didn't know where I was going apart from New York and I didn't know what I was going to do when I got there, I was on a thirty day visa that I planned to let run out and overstay.

I boarded the plane to New York at Manchester airport and flew across the Atlantic to JFK airport. It was night time when I arrived and as I approached the customs I again had the dilemma as to what to say to the customs officer, it was less formal then Tel Aviv and as I approached the customs officer he didn't give me much of a chance to speak he said "Are you here for a holiday" as he looked through my heavy bag, I said "Yes" and he just zipped up my bag, smiled and motioned me through the gate, it was that simple, no fuss no questions. I left the terminal and not having a clue as to where I was going to go I noticed a bus parked outside with New York written on the front and decided to board it, it was going to central station in Manhattan and as I boarded I was charged thirteen dollars, I got the impression I was being ripped off by the young black standing outside the bus but didn't say anything, this was a whole new ball game, I had around ten dollars left and nowhere to turn. The bus arrived at central station and I got off. I looked for the nearest bar and saw an Irish bar not far away, I walked in and bought a coke at the packed bar, I had stopped drinking some time prior to this after having my drink spiked with something in a bar in Liverpool as well as deciding that I had never really liked the taste of the stuff in the first place, so I didn't drink anymore. It was late at night and I was resigned to the fact that I was going to be sleeping outside this night and for how many more I wasn't aware. I still had the option of returning home on the return flight in thirty days but what was the point. Leaving the bar after one drink I spent the night standing in a cold shop doorway with my heavy bag at my feet. Still trying to formulate a plan of action I had decided to see if there was any form of shelter available when the sun came up, I had enough money for a pouch of tobacco and that was it. Sunrise came and I started to make plans to find some shelter, I was lost, but had decided to go to a solicitors to try and gain some information surrounding shelter. I was lucky. I was directed to a homeless outreach worker in an office block. I walked in and explained my situation, not hiding anything I told her the truth about who I was and unfazed she offered me some assistance saying I was lucky to get in. She had given me a referral to a homeless shelter on First Avenue. I was appreciative and told her so. I had no money for food or anything. I made my way to First Avenue over the other side of Manhattan and checked in at the security desk. I very quickly became aware that it was all black people and I was the only white man there. It didn't bother me I just had not been in that situation before. I checked my bag in for a weapons search. The security guard unzipped my bag and pulled out a sledgehammer and nearly laughed, I was close to laughing as well, the security at the airport had not picked up on it for some reason. He said "What are you doing with this?" I just half laughed and said "It's a long story" He confiscated it and said I could have it back on leaving. In my idiocy when I was packing my bag I had put the sledgehammer in as some sort of evidential necessity, it was the hammer I had thrown around the living room that had been seen by Bruce Willis and the American General before going into Iraq. I know realised how ridiculous it actually was. I was out of luck on the equality scale there though, it was a catholic shelter and everything was based around that, I couldn't get away from them, even at street level I was within their grasp. It had an eleven o'clock curfew and you had to resign for your bed every night or you lost it. For the next couple of months I just survived there, the food was very basic but sustained me. I used to go for walks during the day, mainly around central park and playing pool in the pool room of an evening gave me something to occupy me. One evening whilst playing I was spotted by a black man who was called "T" He invited me up onto the top floor to play on a better table with better competition saying I was quite good, I accepted his offer and spent a lot of time playing pool up on the top floor. After a couple of months it was summer, summer in New York was lovely. I used to go and sit in central park in the afternoon. One afternoon whilst I was sitting on a grassy knoll overlooking all of the people walking past, I became aware of someone watching me with a smile on his face, I looked closer and it was someone looking very much like Brad Pitt. He was just standing there watching me, I got up and left, I wasn't playing this game, was it recognition? I believe it was yes.

I started to consider my options and surrounding who I was there where not many, I had heard that if you stayed in the country illegally for five years you then gain citizenship and can work, but five years was a long time, if I could get the story out surrounding who I was it may be easier and this was America, right! Freedom of speech and all that, I decided to try and do something about what had gone on and what was looking like what was going to continue going on. I first thought I would contact a solicitor or lawyer as they are called to see if there was anything legal I could do given I was out of the Windsor domain and the conspiracy would not reach this far given the American "Way" and the freedom of their press, supposed. I made an appointment with a lawyer and went in to see him, he was Jewish and I thought it a bonus as I may gain more understanding for miraculous events backed up with the covert perversion I had been under. He sat and listened and then after I had finished started shrugging his shoulders and sidestepping the issues of perversion and being watched with phone taps, he said it would be very difficult, something I already knew. I thanked him and left the office in dismay. I was also aware that the evidence I had, as a Protestant with it, I had a duty to my faith to produce it and not give up on getting it out to the other Protestants in ignorance of anything untoward going on in the first place. In short they had to be informed, there had to be redress and judgement as well as justice and in this instant it was coming from a King. I then had another idea. I drafted a letter to the New York Times and in it I stated my identity and the miracle I had worked and did they want an interview? I hand delivered it and returned the next day to speak to Laurie Goodstein the reporter I had addressed it to. I patiently waited outside for her to come and speak to me and after a couple of hours I returned to the front desk to ask if I could speak to her. He told me to wait and after another couple of minutes a security guard who's man management skills had been finely tuned deep in the bowels of a Borneo swamp came out and walked up to me and strong armed me off the pavement telling me to leave, this was the American free press looking for new stories and news stories, I walked away. Not to be deterred I then decided to try The New York Daily Post. I wrote a more in depth letter to a news reporter there stating that I was George W Bush's "Noble cause" and it included miracles, I explained what had happened at the New York Times and said I hoped to gain some sort of an interview with a view to telling my story. I again hand delivered it and then again returned the next day to gain some sort of a response. I waited down in the lobby and asked them to phone up the reporter and inform her I was here to speak to her. After a few minutes I was directed to a house phone and she was on the other end, apologetic and understanding she declined an interview, she didn't give any reason and I didn't ask for one, it was polite and understanding. As polite as it was I was still in the same position. Was there a Protestant body I could go to? I considered the possibility and checked the phone book, with the covert surveillance and phone taps I was as much as being held hostage for my power, basically the power of truth and miraculous judgement. All of this was very convenient for the Windsor's. I checked the phone book and looked for any Protestant organisations in New York. I found one, got the address from the phone book and took a trip down there. I walked in and said I wanted to speak to someone in authority from the Protestant faith. I was then informed that they where all Catholics at the place. I was shocked and told them so, it was a misrepresentation. I was lost, there was no redress for it and no justice, how big was it and how big was the organisation I was unaware, but I knew the kind of people involved and the kind of pull they had. For the time being I resigned myself to a life of famed isolation. I continued playing pool with "T", Slim, and two other black guys at the shelter and going for walks to pass the time, by now my flight ticket home had expired and I was illegal. No one seemed to be bothered, no one actually asked too much, so common is it over there.

One night whilst playing pool, I lost track of time and missed the eleven o'clock bed signing, I got down to the office a couple of minutes late and was informed I had lost my bed and was being transferred to wards island veterans of America homeless shelter near Harlem. I went back into the pool room and informed Slim "T" and the others of what had happened, they panicked for me saying it was a nightmare down there as it was right next to Harlem and stabbings took place regularly. Slim told me to come down to the office with him and stated my case to the clerk saying "The niggers down there will cut him up, you can't send him down there" It was to no avail, I was told to pack my bag and given a bus ticket to go immediately. Not knowing what to expect I said my goodbyes to "T" Slim and the others and left, I didn't bother picking up the hammer and left it there. I got on the bus and took a trip to Wards Island near Harlem. On arrival I gave them the relevant information from First Avenue and I was checked in. It was basic, the dormitories where for around fifty people with brick partitioning and a shower block adjoining. There where more white people than I expected and it wasn't as bad as I had been expecting and told it was going to be. It was nearly Christmas now and I didn't even have any money to contact my children with a letter or a Christmas card, all I could do was think of them. I missed them terribly. I knew what it was like without a father. There where regular stabbings at the shelter but for the most part I kept myself to myself and didn't bother anyone. The winter seemed to take an age to pass and it was soon spring. Feeling a little better in the sun I decided to try something else. I began to draft a letter to the Catholic Church given it was a Catholic conspiracy, voicing my concerns and stating the fact that I was a Protestant and they where not going to get away with it, further stating the possibility for war. I took my time writing it getting all of the paper from my case worker and borrowing a pen. By the time the summer arrived it was over thirty pages long and ready to be delivered, I finished it off with the lines, "I have just been told I do not exist please deal with this" I had been told on my revelation to a Muslim case worker at the shelter as to who I was that I did not exist.

I walked into the Catholic Cathedral on Fifth Avenue New York and approached the desk at the front. A woman was working behind it and I told her I needed to speak to a Priest, asking what it was about I informed her it involved a miraculous matter and perversion, I said I had a document that I needed to deliver and that it was somewhat important. She asked me to hand it over saying she would make sure that the Priest got it. I said I would call back in a few days and see what he had to say about it. I had addressed all of the issues surrounding the gross perversion and perverse invasion of my life inclusive of miracles along with the covert fame making game that was going on. Within it I also stated that "With all my heart and soul I am not your enemy and bear you no ill will but you can not get away with this" A couple of days later I again walked along to The Cathedral on Fifth Avenue. This time I walked straight in and made my way to the office and the door was ajar. In the office was a New York cop and the Priest was sitting at his desk with the letter on the table before him, the cop was standing beside the Priest and leaning over the table looking at the document. As I was standing there he said to the Priest "What are you going to do about it" The Priest said "I don't know" I withdrew back into the lobby and sat down and waited, after a few minutes the woman said the Priest would be available soon. He eventually came out and ushered me into his office. He immediately became very defencive and evasive and for the most part refused to even discuss it, I was disgusted, I was being stonewalled. I explained that because of who I was and what was being done I would have to deal with it myself, I explained to him that I had been as much as forced onto the street and had to leave my own children and country because of it. I was wasting my time even talking to him. I then left the office in disgust at the so called Holy mans attitude when faced with the reality of miracles. Now, I am fully aware that state visits are planned months ahead, not long after this Pope John Paul the 2nd on a state visit to America visited the same Cathedral on Fifth Avenue in New York, given the gravity of the document I handed in to the Priest I am curious as to whether it actually was coincidental, knowing the truth in this and it's gravity, I would later on have reason to believe it wasn't coincidental. It had gone that far through the ranks in a short space of time. I was talking about miracles and truth. Liverpool football club also turned up in New York playing A.S Roma but I considered that coincidental or would allow it to be, even though it was very unusual.

The paranormal or miraculous events had subsided for the time being. I wasn't praying to God and for the most part was just surviving in limbo at the shelter. I was very much in the wilderness. One particular night at the shelter I was having a shower when I heard what sounded like someone having a heart attack outside the shower cubicle. I washed the soap out of my eyes and stepped out of the shower. There was an old Puerto Rican man lying on the floor, it took me a few seconds to take in the scene, he was being cradled by one black youth and attended to by another, my eyes where focused on the old man in his seventies lying there.

Standing naked I took in the rest of the scene, I looked to my left and the black youth cradling him was wearing a ski mask, the other black youth who was also wearing a ski mask was going through his pockets, all of this was in a space of seconds, the two youths saw me and ran out of separate doors in the shower block. To my surprise, the old man like a two year old, got up and chased after them. I was standing there naked and dripping wet, I got dried and went out back into the dormitory to run into the security that had been called. They questioned me as to what had happened and I told them. I was then taken into the office and questioned again, I was asked what they looked like and I said I didn't know and before I could elaborate the staff member said "Why, because we all look alike?!" I said "No, they where wearing ski masks but I can tell you what distinctive clothing they where wearing" All of the security cameras had been switched off and they had stolen a couple of hundred dollars off the old man, it had been planned. I asked if the police where going to be called and they said no they where not going to call the police, I got the impression it was because I had witnessed the incident. That is the way it was, the stabbings for the most part had subsided but had been regular. Another occasion involved me and an incident that would lead to stalking through central park. I was lying on my bed when a Catholic Puerto Rican called Jose Morgez walked across from his bed and started ranting and raving about me waking him up, I hadn't but couldn't understand what it was all about, it gained everyone's attention so loud was it, he then slapped me across the head, at which point I swung my legs off the bed to address the situation and to find out what his problem really was and he turned tail and ran out of the dormitory, he returned a couple of minutes later standing behind two security guards who walked towards my bed to see me and they asked me what was going on, someone said "He hasn't done anything" With that the security guards left. Fighting in the shelter was the last thing I wanted and he was standing some way away by now so I left it. He then began ranting in Puerto Rican and finished off in English that the Masons had killed his brother, I didn't have a clue what he was on about, he then lowered his tone and said to his friend next to him that "It is a way of gaining information, watch him!" Whether he knew who I was and what sort of game he was playing I am unaware of but I was very much alone in the situation. He may have been trying to gain "Street cred" I ignored it for the most part until whilst going for a walk through central park I became aware of a stalker following me through the park, it hadn't been the first occasion so it wasn't a coincidence. I was going to have to deal with it myself, so I took a turn off the path and into the woods in Central park to see if he followed, he was a black in his mid thirties, he followed me, I was now aware of how serious the situation was becoming, I was this big and I was who I said I was, maybe to big. I walked over to some rocks and waited on the top of them for him to show himself, just then a woman who was walking her dog came through the bushes, I was looking a little bit suspicious. I got up and walked back down towards the path with her close behind. Sitting behind a rock below was the black who had been following me, I glared at him and he knew I was onto him. After that I avoided Central Park and sometimes walked through the markets in Harlem but for the most part I confined myself to walking along the East River and sitting near the gardens of the Mayors house. Another Christmas was coming up and I wasn't looking forward to it. I considered leaving, but where was I to go, I thought about returning to Great Britain, but even if I wanted to which at this point I didn't, how was I going to get there? I could have turned myself in as an illegal I suppose but for what? To go back to all of the aforementioned! That is the position I was in.

CHAPTER 10

Santa Monica.

Los Angeles.

It was coming up to another Christmas and I didn't feel like spending it there alone without my family, I missed the children. It was harder that time of year. I managed to get a bus pass from my care worker at the shelter and packed my bag, I had formed some sort of an idea about going to the airport but hadn't thought it through. I hadn't even decided where I was going to go other than the airport. I got on the bus to the airport and when I arrived I found myself going over to a phone to make a phone call back to Britain, I reversed the charges and a friend picked up the phone and accepted the charges. It had been nearly two years since I had had contact with anyone who knew me, I had refrained due to possible monitoring but another reason was not knowing what to say. I told him where I was and he listened, but wasn't interested. I said goodbye and put the phone down. I didn't know what to do or how to get any money. I then noticed people paying money for baggage carts, they where paying three dollars a go from a machine outside of the terminal and check in area, whilst the check in area had "Smart Carts" all over the place freely available. I did a quick equation and walked over to one of the unused and disguarded carts and took it out to the payment machine. I waited for someone to walk up to pay for a new cart and offered it for sale at two dollars. It was accepted and I was on to something, there was no security covering it so I again went back into the terminal and got another cart, again selling it at the machine for two dollars. Why none of the other homeless people had thought of it I do not know? It was easy money. After around an hour or so I had nearly one hundred dollars. Another half an hour and I had around another forty dollars. I started getting some looks from one of the staff behind a counter in the terminal, not being sure as to whether he was onto me I stopped. I had began to formulate a plan to gain enough money to travel to Los Angeles and a warmer climate I decided it was too risky to continue and anyway $140 for an hour and a half's work wasn't to bad. I actually thought it would be enough money for a cross country coach ticket to California. I left the airport and got on the train to the coach terminal and asked for a ticket to California, it was too much money I only had enough to get me as far as Chicago. I decided to book the ticket and get the coach to Chicago and hitch it from there, the price of the ticket only left me with a few dollars so I would be travelling from Chicago without food or money. I boarded the coach and set off for Chicago and when I arrived it was freezing with blustery snow being blown around, I asked directions to and headed for the nearest trucking depot. On my arrival I started asking around for a ride going to the West coast, I hadn't made any hitching signs with the direction on so I was very much ill prepared and it was to cold to start making signs outside now. I eventually got a lift heading towards the West coast in a round and about way. Trusting the truckers to know what they where talking about when they suggested the best place to drop me for the next leg of my hike. The first truck driver tried to get me a "Train" going, this involved me being picked up by various truckers as I was dropped off and was arranged over the C.B radio. It was to no avail and I resigned to taking pot luck at my drop off points. My longest wait was a few hours and at one drop off point near a motorway slipway it was night time and very cold, noticing a small shop nearby I walked across and asked if I could stand inside to get warm. I explained I was hitch hiking to California and was cold tired and hungry. The woman behind the counter told me to go into the back and get some sleep. I was grateful and did, after around twenty minutes two police officers walked in and asked me for I.D, she had phoned the police. I offered them my passport and they checked for anything outstanding, they returned it without a problem and left. I slept for another hour or so and then resumed my journey in the cold night, trucks where flying past and it wasn't a very good place to hitch, dark and badly lit. After around four hours Victor Nogalez stopped and offered me a ride, he asked me where I was going and I told him Los Angeles California, he said "You are in luck, I am going all the way" Relieved and tired I climbed in, It would have been the longest leg of the journey as well. He was a nice guy stopping to buy me a good meal after which I climbed in the back of the cab and slept for eighteen hours. He was surprised at the length of time I had slept. I had been on the road for over two days without sleep. We arrived in Los Angeles in daytime and to bright sunshine, it was a pleasant surprise. It had taken me just over three days to hitch across America. I said thank you and got out of the van not knowing what the hell I was going to do next. My first port of call was going to have to be some sort of homeless facility. I started walking towards the beach which was Santa Monica. It was around six miles, but was still early and I had plenty of time, I picked up an old shopping trolley to put my heavy bag in, not realising at the time it was actually illegal to do. I never got stopped. I arrived in

Santa Monica in late afternoon and contacted the first homeless person I saw and asked for directions to the nearest homeless facility. I was directed to St Joseph's, another Catholic facility. It didn't open again until the next morning so I would have to go hungry for the night. I walked around the town and got my bearings, not knowing if there actually where any shelters available. It got late and I eventually went and got some sleep on the beach. The next morning I walked down to St Joseph's and put my name down for one of the free meals provided in the afternoon. There was a psychologist there that everyone had to speak to, to be involved in the centre. You didn't have a choice basically. I went there on a daily basis sleeping out on or near the beach most nights in the warm air. When my turn came to go in and speak to Blake Vienne the psychologist I went in and was basically asked what I was doing there, seeing no reason to lie I began to explain to her what had happened, I went into some depth and she listened intently, I even addressed the issue surrounding my immortality and the accident going into some detail, I also addressed the issues surrounding the conspiracy and explained why I had left my home children and country. So well did I explain it along with nobility, even as a psychologist she was left open mouthed and speechless. She believed me without any further questioning and was quite shocked at the revelations I had offered her. As I left the room, Steve one of the two black security guards started goading me saying as he walked behind me out of the building in a loud voice "Dead man walking, dead man" He had been listening in to the conversation and my explanation, so he now knew who I was in his keyhole perversion. The two security guards over the next couple of months became quite threatening and not knowing why, I again kept myself to myself. They would posture with me and body language was threatening as well, although to be fair it wasn't just me they where doing it to, I thought little of it until one day whilst I was sitting outside on the patio I couldn't help overhear a conversation between Andre' the second black security guard and someone else. He said "I don't doubt he has sat beside Christ, but what I am saying is, you have to threaten!" He was referring to me, someone had obviously taken issue with the way I was being treated and he was explaining his "Game" to them and the way he operated. Now, this was curious to me as I had not even addressed the issue of Jesus Christ with the psychologist so whoever it was who he had the conversation with knew an awful lot about me as I had not made that common knowledge because of how unbelievable it was. I didn't discuss visions or being in anyone's presence with anyone for the most part, it was something I did not fully understand and didn't even know if and when I was having them unless I noticed something like the T.V not even being plugged in confirming I had had a vision. I may have been having them all of my life without realising, so again, I didn't discuss them and again, whoever it was knew both my identity and an awful lot about me. After I heard the conversation, I walked out from the patio to see who it was that had complained about my treatment and they had gone. The bottom line was someone had put the word out on who I was, if they didn't already know. It was a nightmare of a perverted monitoring of a conversation I had had with a psychologist. He was incidentally, talking about operating to a gang formula of threat to gain anger that incorporated witchcraft. Something, as I have said, I am not going to delve into here, although I have had it done to me. I needed somewhere to put my bag and broached the subject with Blake the psychologist. She had put my name down on a list at a place called "Swashlock" It was a small storage facility near the Santa Monica police station. You could get coffee and small amounts of food as and when it was available, but most importantly I now had somewhere to store my bag and that was a big freedom of burden. There was another facility just around the corner called O.P.P.C. It was another homeless facility, after a few months I had learned where to go to get food as and when the places provided it so I wasn't going hungry. There was a shelter available a bus ride away at an "Armoury" in Culver City, they opened it up in the winter and colder months, I stayed there on some occasions but for the most part I avoided the crush on the bus and slept outside in the warm air. Again, I was just surviving and not bothering anyone, going for food at the allocated times and places and spending the nights on a grass hill outside the Casa Del Mar hotel near to the Santa Monica pier. On one night I was awoken to two police officers I would later find out where officer Martinez and Ltnt Perez. They asked me for I.D and questioned me as to what I was doing here, here being America. Being aware they where both Catholic's I was cautious, but told them basically that I had to leave Britain after working a miracle. This aroused there curiosity and they wanted to know more, I kept any further explanation brief. They then gave me an "Illegal camping" ticket and left. I spent most of the time sitting around and as I have said just surviving. One day whilst at the "Swashlock" facility, I was sitting outside when a woman called Lee walked over and introduced herself, she was another Catholic. She became very strange talking in riddles and saying things that where familiar to me and my situation and then it became apparent she knew who I was. She stood up and opening her jeans she exposed herself making it clear that she wanted to have sex with me. I was sitting down against a wall with my legs stretched out and she came and sat astride my legs and then grabbing my head, she pulled it towards hers and said "We need the Windsor's" and started laughing, I got out of the situation by throwing her off to one side and I left. It was becoming increasingly obvious I was going to have to do something, but what? I had no where to turn. I had no money whatsoever, my children didn't even know where I was and I was undergoing a form of kidnapping in the public domain. I again resigned myself to the fact that there was nothing I could do and no where I could go. I continued to just survive until one night whilst sleeping near the Castle Del Mar officer Martinez and another low ranked officer ran around from my blind side shouting and waving guns in the air. I was sitting bolt upright by the time they got to me. They had their guns on me without safety as the red laser light was in my eyes. They where laughing and motioning their guns at me, officer Martinez then said something that exposed himself as being fully aware of who I was, he said "You do not exist!" as he waved the gun in my face. He had just quoted the last lines of the document that I handed in to the Catholic Cathedral in New York. They where fully aware of what they where doing and who they where doing it to, they then ran off laughing. I packed up my things and left the area and whilst walking down past the sea front they pulled up along side me in the patrol car and repeated the taunt "You do not exist" I shouted back over that that was the biggest mistake he had ever made and I was going to deal with it. He drove off. But he was right, I didn't exist in any domain, apart from a covert one. In reality I was a very famous man indeed, maybe to big for the Catholic's. They had made me massive in song and political rape and usage. But in the cold light of peoples innocent ignorance, I was just a mad man. It was evil. Not long after this I was again asleep by the hotel. I was covered in my sleeping bag and had my head covered as well, I sensed something was not right and poked my head out of the sleeping bag to see Ltnt Perez standing over me with a gun pushed against his crotch with one hand over the other in an assassin position. Another occasion involved two separate officers whilst I was sitting in the gazebo near the hotel, again it was late at night and very dark and there was no one about. The two officers pulled up outside the gazebo and got out of the car, as they approached the gazebo one of the officers drew his firearm and as he did so he was bouncing around as if he was in the middle of a bank job and looking all around for any witnesses, there was no humour in this incident, I was seriously concerned that I was going to be shot so serious was there behaviour, again they where both Latino and Catholic, I decided to stay away from the area for a while. I changed my area where I sat, it was summer now and hot so I used to walk along what is called The Palisade's nearer to the pier. I would find a vacant palm tree to sit under and spend the day there just sitting there. The incidents with the police gave me reason to consider it prudent to try to find shelter indoors at the armoury. It meant a queue and fighting a crowd of homeless to get a seat. One particular night I was in the armoury watching T.V and George Bush's state of the union speech was being aired, in it he made reference to "Sitting under a palm tree in Santa Monica" I thought it a little bit of a strange thing to say. For you, to read me pick something out like that and expect it to be believed as none coincidental is understandably harder to believe, but when some time after that Tony Blair turned up in Santa Monica not more than six hundred yards from where I was sleeping and given the rest of my life, it ceases to be coincidental. Yes of course in your eyes it could be coincidental. Personally, I doubt it given who I was. Anyway later evidence and incidents would clear my paranoia with undeniable direct hits.

I stayed in the armoury in Culver City for a while but it was difficult, you where tied to times and standing around in a queue for hours waiting for a bus that didn't always turn up. I decided to move back outside to sleep and resumed my usual place on the grass near the hotel and gazebo. I set up my sleeping bag and got in, soon after two other people came across and set up to go to sleep, it was a man and a woman in their thirties I later found out it was Sean and Leslie. They sat for a while just looking over at me and I turned over and went to sleep. They returned on numerous nights and became regular. One afternoon whilst sitting outside the hotel on the grass, a group of people came behind me and set up some sort of a tent so I moved out of their way and sat far to the right. It was some sort of an audition and a group of people gathered around near the front of the tent and started clapping and shouting as if on camera in a show. I looked across to see this but otherwise paid little attention to it. Then after a few minutes a woman with a clip board came out of the tent and walked over towards where I was sitting, she walked in circles very close tome and then pulled out her phone as if to answer it. She put it to her ear and looking at her clipboard said "Who? Alan Sloan" No, I wasn't imagining it, someone was trying to get me to dance for them, the entertainment industry. I hadn't misheard my name it was definitely me she was referring to. I ignored it and her. I wasn't playing this game either. I again slept near the hotel and this particular night the man and the woman, Leslie and Sean came up onto the same level of grass as me and said "Hi" I replied with the same "Hi" and left it at that and turned over to go to sleep, I then heard some groans and moans, I looked around and it was the woman, Leslie she was in her sleeping bag and rolling around saying "Oh I want to fuck it, I want to fuck it" She was referring to me and climaxing. With that her boyfriend came straight over to where I was lying and grabbed me by the throat, I grabbed hold of his hand as best as I could and wrestled it from my throat and used it to pull myself up and out of the sleeping bag. I then beat him up, I didn't have a choice, he hadn't left me any, he had and was attacking me. It is the last thing you want when sleeping outside so you can close your eyes in relative safety. You don't need or want any enemies. It is too easy to get to you. He made that clear with his next statement of "Ill stab you in your sleep" He then approached me again to attack, so I had to beat him up again, they where both Catholic's and at that point I was not aware of the fact that they also knew who I was. I left it at that, they where trouble. A little later a crowd of other homeless people walked past down below and the male started shouting across to them trying to start another fight. Now in danger of arousing the company of the police I decided to move and packed up my things to move, as I did so the female mouthed the words, thank you, for beating up her boyfriend!? I went for a walk for a while thinking they would leave eventually. I walked for around half an hour and then made my way back, safe sleeping places are hard to find and this was mine. I approached the small grass hill unseen by them and began to roll out my sleeping bag on the other side, as I looked up I was in time to see them give each other a high five and say "All thing's are nearly naked and open" It was another direct reference to the quatrain, they knew who I was, or to be more precise they knew what was being done to me. All things naked and open meaning the truth is nearly out to be seen. A few nights later I was sleeping in the same area when the police arrived again, this time I was arrested on an outstanding illegal camping warrant, I was taken to the police station In Santa Monica and I demanded a phone call. I was given one and the desk sergeant phoned up the British Consulate as I had asked him to and when the line was ready I was put on the phone, I told them I had a problem and that I was a British citizen, I gave them my name and told them the situation they said they would phone back, they never called back. I was kept locked up for a day and released. That is the sentence for homeless trespass, a one day prison sentence. I wasn't aware of that but it did give me insight into the British Consular attitude to a citizen in need of help. It wouldn't be the first time.

I decided on another course of action, I went back down to St Joseph's where they allowed you to make local calls and I phoned up the consulate in Los Angeles myself, I again spoke to Caroline and informed her of my identity historic. I then told her that I expected some sort of assistance, I had told her most of what was going on and didn't much care who was listening at or in St Joseph's, I finished off by saying if I wasn't offered any assistance I would have no option other than to release information that would make them wish they had, I was talking about people being watched in their own homes and miracles etc. I asked her if she understood and she said that she did. This was horrendous my whole life was being destroyed as well as any life in conjunction with my children. I put the phone down after informing her of my whereabouts. How the hell was I going to do it? There was no way they where going to help me, to help me was to admit it and to admit it was to admit the House of Windsor was finished and guilty of both impotence and inability as well as possible complicity in the ongoing cover up. I had to get this out and I had to write it down, it would take an age. Explanation and evidence that at times and at best was vague and thin, even though there was researchable undeniable bulk and visible evidence, was it enough? It was asking a lot at times but I had to try.

After a couple of days there was still no contact by or from the British Consulate. How was I going to get it out? I had no choice now, writing it out in letter form was not an option even if I had any paper which I didn't. Still wondering what to do, a couple of nights later whilst walking along the dark shoreline of the beach in Santa Monica Someone said "Hello" I looked up to see a young woman sitting there and I walked across and said "Hello" I sat down next to her and we started talking, the conversation turned to where I was from and what I was doing here so I just told her the story and then told her the predicament of trying to get the evidence out, she said "Have you got an email account, you could try the internet to write it down" I hadn't thought of that, it had possibilities, even though I couldn't type and didn't know my way around the internet, surely it wouldn't take to long to learn. She shared a glass of wine with me and we made arrangements to meet the next day at the library so she could teach me the basics of the internet she gave me her email address as "Summer Lee Cooper" I arrived the next day at the library and waited for some time, little did I realise at the time but it was the wrong library. We had missed each other and I never saw her again, she was nice. But now I had a plan, although it would take some time at least I had a way of exposing them. I walked into the main library in Santa Monica and had to produce my passport for a library card, I got one no problem but was informed that you could only have an hour a day, with my basic typing skills which where none existent it would take some time. I asked the librarian to show me how to open an email account and he kindly did taking his time to show me. On opening the account I started writing it from the beginning. If people where aware of who I was I am unaware of it. I had found a dollar in the street the day after and was there as the library opened the next morning, I immediately bought a floppy disc and asked the librarian to show me how to use it and store the evidence on it. He did and I was away, I was there every morning for around a month writing the evidence down and feeling quite pleased with my self as it was going so well. The one morning I walked into the library and inserted the disc and all of the information had been wiped or had just disappeared, I was devastated, a month of work, one hour every morning religiously, just gone. I didn't at that point think anything suspicious about it, it was later on that I would think back and wonder. I decided not to use a disc again, even if I had the money to buy another one and I didn't. I then started to use my email account, I kept it in the letter draft and restarted writing it all over again, it was disheartening but necessary. I was in there every day again for one hour only, it was going slow and my typing wasn't up to much, I was also to make a lot of mistakes in it as well, something that would later bother me as I sent it global. Though at this time not knowing how I was going to get it out, but realising the necessity of writing it I continued every day religiously. One day after finishing at the library I even contacted the Mormons at the local church, it was a waste of time.

I was still sleeping near the Castle Del Mar hotel and one night whilst I was in my sleeping bag, Leslie the woman who "Wanted to fuck it" came over and sat very close to me, she had been drinking and looking for

Sean, or so she said asking me if I had seen him, she then made a pass at me, she was attractive and I responded. We had sex right there on the grass under the tarpaulin cover I had for my sleeping bag. We spent the night together. It was welcome company for me. The next morning we woke up and I said I was leaving for some coffee at the "Swashlock" facility and she responded saying she was going to sleep a little longer, I got up and left. It wasn't until the next day that I saw her and she walked past without responding to me, it was sometime later that another man walked past me and said "Nobody rapes Leslie!" I quickly realised what she had done, she had instigated sex with me, given me unrequested oral sex and then shouted rape to get me in trouble possibly physical. I then started to give all of the Catholic's a wide birth, something I had done for a while unless in necessity, but now I was more cautious, the lies they can tell. You can get seriously beaten up at street level for something like that and she was aware of it. I had another problem at O.P.P.C when I was attacked without reason by a black whilst in the shower queue. He had just come into the centre and walked to the front and demanding to be next rounded on me, a fight ensued and he then ran off out of the centre, unbeknown to me the police had been called and where waiting outside when I left the building. They approached me and asked me what had happened, I explained the situation to them and they became aggressive asking me what I was going to do about it?! I said "Nothing" and stated that it was me who had been attacked, they where both Catholic's and asked me what I was doing over there, I briefly explained a difficult explanation stating that I was a Protestant and they became more aggressive, at this point I was already considering travelling or trying to travel back to Britain. I had focused on the evidence coming out eventually via the internet so was feeling a little more confident in my future. I explained that to them and one of the officers then asked me "Are you going to burn woman and children?" I said "What!?" In disbelief and with that one of the officers lunged at me, threw my arms behind my back and tripped me up onto the pavement forcing my face into the concrete slab. The other officer then began jumping up and down on my back, the other officer again pushed my head hard into the pavement causing a lot of cuts and bruises, by this time a crowd had stood watching this all going on and they became nervous, so I was cuffed and thrown into the back of the patrol car. They quickly got in and drove around the corner where there where no people, they then stopped the car and left me in the back and got out of the car, they waited a minute and then a fire truck turned up and they got me out of the car, they had damaged my ribs and my lower back so at this point I was in severe pain, I had serious cuts and bruises on my face and was bleeding. One of the officers from the fire truck produced a camera from somewhere and asked me if I wanted him to photograph the evidence of my injuries, I said "Yes" He then began photographing me, so bad where my injuries. I was taken into the hospital by ambulance and admitted for x rays to my back and chest. At this point or the point of arrival I was marched into the hospital with the words of one officer stating that I was a coward, I said to him "Take the cuffs off and well see who the coward is!" Then looking around there where no less than SEVEN police officers around me as I was escorted into the accident and emergency, I was handcuffed with both hands to either side of the bed with chest injuries, all of the officers where stationed outside, it was ridiculous, SEVEN officers for one homeless man. I was in severe discomfort and pain and at this point could not even get off the trolley to get a proper x ray done. The officer who made the taunt of "Coward" was laughing and joking. So I shouted over to him and got his attention, I was furious, I spoke to him surrounding who I was and said that whatever happened this was coming out and he was now a major part of the attack, I went into a few other things surrounding miracles for the benefit of him and the others and he nearly burst out crying, his bottom lip started going. He didn't know where to put his face or what to say in reply. It was just an unnecessary attack on an innocent man who had been attacked himself. They knew what they where doing and I made sure they knew who they had done it to. I then began shouting all over the accident and emergency as to what was going on and to remember it. The whole place heard me, I made sure of it. Still in agony they brought down a portable x ray machine and x rayed me on the bed. The x rays came back clear and I was then taken to the cells in Santa Monica and checked in, I was finger printed and had a swab taken for D.N.A, when the officer asked for my next of kin I said George W Bush, he looked at me curious and asked again, I repeated it, he shrugged his shoulders and filled out the form as I had stated. Soon after a waggon appeared in the station and I was ferried to Los Angeles County jail. I was seriously worried "What where they going to concoct?" We where all x rayed on our arrival before going into circulation. I was put into circulation and was placed into a dorm with other prisoners, After a couple of days I was called out for another x ray as my original had gone missing, I was to spend nearly ten days in there before I was summoned to go before a judge. Not being told any charges or anything or even how long I would be on remand, it was very worrying. I had to try and get a pen and paper to state my case in case I was being railroaded by them.

I managed to get some scrap paper on the morning I was told to get ready for court. We where ferried around from cell to cell and I was trying to gain enough time to write the statement, it was hard but I just about managed to finish it. We where then placed into a waggon shackled and chained and driven to the law courts. I had spent around ten days in prison for nothing. The law courts had a series of rooms for waiting prisoners to speak to a solicitor or lawyer. We where taken in three at a time to speak to a solicitor. My turn came and I asked to speak to him in private he touched his nose frantically and called me "A fucking jerk" but allowed me to have a private conversation with him. I didn't want to identify myself in front of other prisoners. I told him who I was and handed him the written document of explanation. I felt relieved that he had received it before the court hearing. I walked into the court hearing and wasn't allowed to speak as usual. I sat and listened and couldn't hear any charges. My solicitor turned to me and said "It is going to be considered as time served" in other words, I had already served my time and I would be released. I was, as I stood up and was about to leave the court room the judge turned to me and said "I hope your mental illness gets better" I wasn't, but how the hell did he know about it in the fist place?! Who was doing this but moreover, who was giving this information out? I left in disbelief. This was a court room in America, without me identifying myself to anyone other than minutes before a hearing. Someone was going to a lot of trouble to convince people of my metal instability or incapacity and I wasn't imagining it.

    I was released back outside and left and headed back to Santa Monica. I was now considering leaving the place, the document was going well and I was getting through it slowly but surely. Whilst sitting under another palm tree one day an officer on a bicycle stopped, leaned over and said "Time to leave" He meant the area and he was right, it was I had contracted and been treated for crabs and scabies several times whilst I was there as well which wasn't nice, the place was rife with them, I had been bitten by a brown recluse spider and spent three days in hospital on a drip as well and on one occasion a Catholic nurse injected an aneurysm into my arm with the words "A little bubble won't hurt you", I had also had my bag stolen from the "Swashlock" facility as well, all of my certification and belongings, but what hurt me the most was the picture of my three children that was taken I was never to get it back, I was glad to be leaving. But where was I to go?

CHAPTER 11

San Francisco

I considered my options that where few without money. I thought if I travelled North up to San Francisco I would be on my way to Canada and decided that would be the best place to go, I just hoped they had the same facilities for homeless up there. I had a fair walk to find a truck stop, it was miles away, I didn't tell anyone I was leaving there was no one to say goodbye to. I got to the truck stop and eventually got a lift up the coast going to San Diego, it was close enough and I could get another lift from there. I was dropped off and the place seemed desolate, it was nearly Christmas again and I was thinking of home such as it was. I managed to find an outreach centre where I could get some food, it was basic and I was told that if I waited until after Christmas I would get a free bus ticket to San Francisco. It sounded good to me and I got my sleeping bag out and waited the two or three days for Christmas to finish. As good as their word after Christmas I was given the money for a bus ticket and I thanked them and set off on the coach. I arrived in San Francisco in the early morning and as usual asked the nearest homeless person where all of the facilities where, I was told and went along to get some food. I found the place looking dirty in comparison to others I had been in the States, when I got to the relevant food place the queue was around the block and then around another corner, I had never seen so many homeless people, it was visibly obvious that drugs where a problem there. Crack Cocaine seemed to be running the streets and the blacks would walk past you and whisper into your ear "Free crack" It was that obvious. Their where also a lot of trans gender people struggling with identities, having serious psychological problems, men with breasts where running the homeless facilities and I found them very discriminatory to people of a heterosexual nature. I took an instant dislike to the place. It wasn't warm or friendly in any concept. Even being homeless didn't make any difference. I mean I don't think being homeless was the reason. It seemed to be to uninhibited, not to be confused with cosmopolitan. This was downtown San Francisco, I had already located the library near the U.N plaza. But I wouldn't get in there for a couple of days. My first priority was a bed. I was going to need one here. The homeless queue's where endless wherever you went for something, I only had a small bag now with very little in since everything was stolen, so storage wasn't a problem, there where woman carrying around suit cases and I felt sorry for them, it must have been hard. Everywhere you go lugging around lots of baggage. For meals, for walks to appointments, it was a chore I had done many times. I entered the queue for a bed as soon as I had eaten just after I got there, they only handed them out for seven day periods, you got a bed for seven days and then had to re apply for another seven days and as I have said their was the trans gender click to deal with. They would visibly hand out beds over your head to other trans gender and homosexual people. It was a little "Clicky" game for them. Again, some of them did have serious problems. But, I was on the homeless circuit. I eventually got a bed for seven days so did not have to sleep outside. I was relieved and checked in. It was a small shelter in downtown San Francisco. It was one floor of a building with camp beds spread out on the lower floor. You could reach out and touch the person next to you whilst you lay on the bed, it slept around fifty people. There was no privacy and no walls. But again, it was free, warm, inside, you got a meal and no one asked too many questions. I was to pick up and get treated for scabies again, three times. The next day I went to the main library to see what it was like rule wise and to continue the document I walked in and produced my passport to gain a library ticket, I got one no problem, a visitors card. I looked around the library and the rules where the same, you got one hour per day, but the difference here was that they had what is called speed computers where you didn't have to book and could queue up constantly for a fifteen minute spell on the internet as often as you liked, as well as your usual one hour on the main terminals. This would be handy. I could write a lot more of the document on a daily basis. I logged on for my first hour and went into my email account, I clicked the button to go into my drafts to continue the document and it wasn't there, it was just gone, no sign of it, I hadn't made a mistake or anything, someone had physically removed it. They had broken into my email account and wiped it from the account, I wasn't fully computer literate but I knew that much. I was furious, months of work just erased and gone. It made the computer disc in Santa Monica being wiped look very suspicious, how they got into my account I wasn't aware but they or someone had got in. Of that I was sure. Dismayed I decided to start again, this kind of thing wears you down and worn down at this point I was. I started to re write the document again in another account with a new password. Like the rest of this, I wasn't imagining it, someone with good reason didn't want this coming out, they didn't mind me talking or writing and monitoring it for their own use either politically or musically for monetary gain or political power. What they didn't want was anyone knowing the truth about what was going on. I was being denied my name and they where trying to stop me proving it.

I restarted the document in the other account, I had to find some sort of safeguard in case the same thing was done again so I opened yet another email account and each day before I signed off I sent a copy out to the other account that I wasn't using and as far as I was aware, no one else was aware of it either. I was to have a lot of problems with my computer crashing all of the time and things I had written being wiped on the restart, at first I thought it coincidental until I noticed that it was only and always my computer terminal that was crashing, wherever I was in the library and whatever terminal I was at. It would constantly crash wiping all of the information I had written. Everyone else's was alright. It wasn't coincidental, over the next few months it was clear it was personal to me. No it wasn't paranoia. I had to type and save very quickly as well as sending out the document. After another few months of virtually being camped out in the library seven days a week typing, the document was nearly finished, within it I had offered an awful lot of evidence and explained how it was a kidnapping in the public domain, I explained how it was risky for me to even approach a woman to talk to in case she was in turn approached behind my back and raped, yes I was being isolated to this extent ("Such alone can prophecy" It means someone totally isolated and alone). I had stopped talking to virtually everyone accept for necessity. The Windsor's had turned up in Washington, and Charles Windsor had turned up in San Francisco talking to the homeless people, personally I do not think it was a coincidental to my being there and the homeless issue he was purportedly addressing was I believe connected to me. Things that where happening where just too coincidental. As I have said the document was nearly finished and ready for me to do something with it, but what? Where would I take it? Would I print it out and just hand it out to people? I certainly didn't have any money for anything of that nature. I had an idea. I would send it out via email. I would gain addresses from the Internet and send it out globally in order to take my name back. Make myself famous basically. It was all I could think of and basically all I could do. I started harvesting emails from the internet, pubs, clubs and bars at first all over Great Britain and globally. I went for San Francisco as well, but they where basically all over the world, someone else, like me, had to have a problem with what was going on. It was evil. Little did I know at that time but my email accounts where being monitored as well. After I harvested the emails I placed them at the bottom of the document so that other people could see how many people globally where also reading it. I contacted the press and got hundreds of email addresses of newspapers globally and locally. All of the British press got a copy of it. I got names where I could and sent out individual copies of it to the relevant people. I had written it too quickly and made a lot of mistakes in both grammar and fact, I wasn't thinking straight through a lot of it, conscious of being monitored. At the top of each email I sent I also put the email address of the White House, The Vatican and Buckingham Palace. They all received a copy. I didn't finish the document there, I kept it going and turned it into a diary of events that I updated and dated on a daily basis. It was basically charting the events and happenings throughout my life in the situation I was being held in.

I didn't receive one single response from any of the emails I sent out unless it was a computer generated response, not one offer of an interview from any of the press, not even a response. I was dumbfounded there had to be some sort of redress for this. Little did I realise at that time that the press had involvement in phone tapping scandals that would come out in due course, I still firmly believe it was as a direct result of the document I was writing, so global was it along with it's undeniable content. It had created a knock on effect allowing people who where having similar things done to them of voicing concerns without fear of accusations of mental illness. In short, they could now say "I have had this done to me as well" By the time the document had ran it's course over the coming months and indeed years it was over 900 pages long and was to have over 37,000 email addresses in it and had been sent out to every nation on earth, every British Embassy and Consulate on the planet, hundreds of other embassies of every country on earth, towns, cities, villages, politicians, world leaders and any other email address I could get my hands on. I also believe the document has played a part in the downfall of the Middle Eastern dictators and is in part way responsible for the "Arab Spring" I sent it out with a covering letter all over the Middle East as well. All over Russia, China and the U.S.A, everyone was to know my name and what was going on. I had to get the document and the evidence out from the circle I was being held in as big as it was. In short, things where happening.

   I had been toying with weather patterns my entire life without even really realising. I would ask for the sun to come out and it would, since a very early age. Cloud busting before even realising there was a name for it. It usually worked, I could predetermine weather patterns and not just locally it went on farther afield. It was a game I played as a child basically and now it was full on hits every time. Stopping rain and moving clouds. It was normal for me, if I didn't like the weather I changed it basically. It is what I used to do when I had finished at the library for the day. It was just another of the many things and events I never discussed with anyone.

CHAPTER 12

Portland, Oregon

It was coming to the end of summer now in San Francisco and the carnivals had been on. The streets had been packed with revellers and people in Sado Masochistic regalia where wall to wall. People in chains and whips abound, I found it a little too hedonistic and distasteful, there where children dotted around as well. It is a very hedonistic city with a lot of visible underlying drug problems and I was thinking of leaving, but the library was ideal for me. Then I bumped in to a woman called Sarah Flurry outside the library who said she was looking for her old boyfriend. We struck up a conversation against my better judgement and wishes. I did not want any contact with a woman because of what was going on, but it was difficult. She said she had a problem with her new boyfriend. He was a black crack dealer and wanted to prostitute her. She said she had done it but didn't want to do it any more and she was going to leave and was looking for someone to leave with, she was very attractive and in spite of that I wasn't that keen to go with her, a lot of homeless had serious problems. I said I was sorry about it and said goodbye and walked back into the library. I was in there a few minutes at one of the speed computers and she came in and found me and we started talking again. She said she wanted me to come with her as she was scared alone, I said I didn't have any money to go anywhere. She said that she would pay and we started getting along alright. Eventually I agreed, I picked up my backpack and we walked to the greyhound coach terminal there and then, she had left everything she owned in the flat with him. We walked up to the desk at the terminal and the woman asked us where we where going to and we hadn't even discussed it. I still had Canada in my sights and thought that Oregon was a step in the right direction, so I said to the girl at the desk "What is the state capitol of Oregon" and she said "Portland" I looked at Sarah and said "Do you fancy it?" She said "Yes o.k" She paid for the tickets and we where soon on our way stopping off and changing once. There had been flood warnings in Portland it had been raining for some time. I was actually watching very little television now if any at all, so I wasn't getting much news from anywhere and not much feedback from the document on any programmes, but where possible I was keeping my ear open for any hits. As we where driving into Portland the rain was heavy so I said to Sarah, "Do you want to stop the rain with me" It was the first time I had ever included anyone in such a thing so private to me was it and I was unsure as to whether it would actually work with a third party involved. She smiled and said "Yes" I said "O.k after me and with me, start singing Here comes the sun by the Beatles" She smiled and we did it quietly in our seats. Ten minutes later the rain had stopped and the floods where averted. I was laughing.

We arrived in the Portland bus terminal and although it was the state capitol it didn't look like a very major city, it seemed out of the way and off the beaten track. I didn't know what we where going to do or where we where going to stay, I was thinking about the usual "Homeless person ask" To find out where all of the facilities where, I wasn't used to having anyone with me. It was then that Sarah asked where the nearest and cheapest hotel was. The man at the desk told us and gave us directions, it wasn't far and we walked there.

When we went in Sarah asked for a double room and was charged around $80 for the night for two, I was later to find out that it was a $17 a night hotel that the homeless used when they got there state benefit, we had been ripped off as strangers. It was basic, a room with a bed and a shower and sink. I was glad of the shower and got straight in. We slept together that night. Sarah had seemed perfectly lucid throughout all of our journey and meeting. We got up the next morning and she needed to go to the post office to get some more money sorted out so we walked there and had a walk about to get our bearings in the new city. After some time walking around we walked back to the hotel. I was beginning to wonder how long this would last, I had no way of gaining any money other than to beg and she couldn't sustain me and her for to long, aside from everything else it wasn't and didn't seem fair. We where sitting in the room that night and she became agitated, she was withdrawing from crack cocaine, I hadn't realised. She was also on medication she hadn't taken. Then she exploded in rage and shouted all over the hotel and through the open window into the street that she didn't want to be on crack anymore and was at a loss as to what to do. It went on for a good few minutes and I was waiting for a knock at the door from the management of the hotel but it didn't come. There was no talking to her to calm her, she then in rage, made reference to me being a King, she knew who I was and hadn't said anything, I later realised she was also Catholic. It was a very difficult situation to deal with, it sounded for all intents and purposes that she was shouting at her crack dealer. ME. We had just got to the city and she was shouting all over the place about crack and addiction. Eventually she calmed down and said that she had just had an "Episode" I had decided that it was to much of an awkward situation to stay in, she was unstable, it was going to be impossible and a split was necessary. I would explain and leave the next morning. The atmosphere was bad for the rest of the night and I just slept, she needed help I was not in a position to and could not give her. The next morning I got up and said I was leaving, she asked me not to but I explained I had no choice, I told her the situation and money wouldn't allow me to stay. I apologised and left the hotel. At least I had a full day to get myself sorted out finding facilities and such. Again, as usual I approached the first homeless person I saw and asked him for information and he was good enough to give it to me. There seemed to be plenty of facilities from what he said and I made my way to one of them. There was only one place for shelter though which could be a problem as the winters in Portland can get pretty cold. I didn't have a blanket or sleeping bag so I needed somewhere inside for the night until I could get some blankets or a sleeping bag from one of the homeless outreach places. I found the place with the beds available on Burnside Avenue and had something to eat and then enquired about shelter. It was a lottery system and you got a ticket each night that was drawn from a hat. Given it was the only shelter and only had around fifty beds in a downstairs dorm, together with the fact that there where at least one hundred people wanting them, it was obvious that there was a good chance I was going to be on the street. The only upshot was that if you didn't get a bed on the lottery they handed out blankets to the unsuccessful at eight o'clock. I was lucky my ticket came up and I got in on the first attempt, the way it worked was, you where allocated a seven day bed on winning the lottery every month, the rest of the time you would only get one bed for one night so you where only guaranteed being off the street for seven days every month. It was going to be cold, winter was coming fast, but at least I had seven days in the shelter to get my bearings, again no one asked me too many questions. I walked downstairs to the basement where the beds where that night and there was a clothing window where you could get items of clothing for free. I thankfully rigged myself out with jeans socks and underwear then I took a shower slept and the next day changed my clothes. Carrying things was a problem so the less you had the better I restricted it usually to a spare pair of jeans if I had them and a clean top. Washing clothes was always a problem with the facilities not usually having that luxury. What they did have was have a bin where you could swap dirty for clean clothes and they would get them washed over a period of time and just recycle them, it worked quite well. The next day I got my bearings a littler better, the place seemed smaller than I had imagined it would be being the state capitol. I located the library in the town centre and it was a relatively small building that had the appearance of an old stately home that had been converted with a double marble staircase, it was "Oldy worldy" It had three floors with computer terminals on every floor, what they didn't have was speed computers so I would be limited to one hour every day to update the now document stroke diary and harvest as many email addresses as I could. It would take longer to do now. Remembering what had happened in San Francisco to my document I was worried at logging in to my account in case it had all gone again although I did have copies in another account. I again used my passport and was given another library ticket. I logged in and everything was fine, feeling confident that I had by this time got enough evidence out at this point I wasn't to worried, if anyone knew who I was they didn't say anything about it, apart from Sarah that is. I finished for the day and stayed at the shelter that night, again keeping myself very much to myself I wasn't talking to anyone. The next day whilst waiting in a food line for dinner I saw Sarah and she came over looking a little lost and I felt very sorry for her. I didn't know what to say and just said "Hi" and she smiled, we started talking and went in to have a meal together. She then left, I saw her the next day walking down the road with another man and after that I was never to see her again. I found Portland to be a nice enough place and the people where friendly enough, it seemed to be a flash back from the old wild west in some places and was a lot slower pace than San Francisco and quieter as well. There where not as many homeless in Portland but there was enough. It was a colder place in the winter and there where not as many homeless facilities as other places I had been so maybe that was the reason. I thought about my children a lot at this point and was missing them terribly and missing them growing up in a very real sense, wondering what they where doing, it was hard. Still not having a penny. I could have asked Sarah for a few dollars to write home, but even if I did now what was I to say? "Dad is living on the streets and working miracles after being accused of being mentally ill" Not a very good boast for a child to a friend is it?! I tried to put it to the back of my mind but couldn't so I prayed for them, safe in the knowledge of answered prayers, it made me feel closer to them.

The staff at the shelters where all friendly, always having a smile for you for the most part, it was a difficult job for them as some of the homeless had serious problems. It was a welcome change from San Francisco. Sleeping outside was always a risk as well. You where open to anyone who had a problem with anything. One homeless man was killed whilst I was there, he was asleep in a shop doorway and someone had walked up to him and smashed his head in with some sort of blunt object. They had hit him once whilst he was asleep and killed him, he wouldn't have known anything about it, that and they where the risks you where taking. The police where at a loss, they didn't know anything for all they knew it could have been another homeless person. There could have been a killer among us, a lot of the homeless carried weapons for that reason. I had taken to carrying a rock in a sock in my coat pocket. My week was up and I had to leave the shelter and sleep outside. All I had was a blanket. I had kept on the lookout for somewhere safe to sleep whilst I was walking around the town. Some people slept outside the shelter but it was noisy and on a long slope on Burnside Avenue, comfort was an issue at the best of times whilst sleeping on concrete. I had kept myself a bit too much to myself. I had missed some information about another homeless facility. It was called "Daywatch" and was a good facility. Drinks where a problem on the street if you didn't have any money, you only got a coffee at meal times twice a day, three if you went for lunch, this place had coffee on tap and was open all day, you could also store a bag there for the entire day which was an added bonus. I walked in and was introduced to Cathy, a member of staff and a lovely woman I was to become friendly with. She really was genuine in her help and compassion for the homeless. They also had computer terminals upstairs which you could use for an hour on a daily basis Monday to Friday. That was great it would mean I would get two hours per day on a computer to get the document out. The place was packed most days and opened at six a.m. The computer invasion didn't or hadn't stopped, I used to get small messages in my account as I was writing that another user was breaking in to my account, it used to come up in a small box on the screen. Another instant was that when someone tried to open or indeed would open another one of my accounts it showed up in the account I was using and I could sit and watch how long they where in the account for before the little yellow smiley face that indicated someone was using one of my other accounts went out. I had for sometime been very angry at what was going on and whilst they hadn't wiped the document from my account as they had done before, they had been into my document account and altered some script in the document and what was now my diary of daily events and miraculous happenings. I had been furious about it for some time and had a lot of literal profanity within it. I wasn't imagining it either there where times when I could actually sit and watch them do it at my terminal. I knew it was the Catholic's. I was still getting it out and there was still a noticeable absence of responses. Where they being wiped from my account before I could log on in the daytime? It was possible.

I had been sleeping outside in a shop doorway for some time now and had put a request in to Cathy for a sleeping bag when one came in from a donation, one eventually came in and I was given it one Friday night when I went in, the facility opened up for three hours on a Thursday and Friday night as well. Working on the computers only lasted two hours a day so I had a lot of time on my hands, alone and isolated I just waited for things to happen and when they did I would place the event in the document as and when it happened, on one occasion whilst I was sitting in what was called the Japanese garden one cloudy autumn afternoon, it was a small shrine along the Potomac River with a few plaques for the Japanese interns in America during the second world war. I was just lying there on my back and feeling a little cold I could see the sun through the hazy grey of the clouds I had always thought or literally sang to bring out the sun and had never done this before. What I did was purse my lips and pointing my head in the direction of the sun behind the haze, I blew, long and hard. I know how ridiculous you may think this but it is actually true, the weather forecast will bear testament to it happening at that time. Within a minute it had started hail stoning and it was caused by me. If you think about the action of blowing cold air into the sky and a rain soaked cloud it would in a literal sense, make sense. But you can not separate the science from the miraculous. Now I know what I have let myself in for there and to a certain extent I would agree with your thoughts. Right up to the point whereby the next day I was lying in the same place under the same weather pattern and did the same thing with exactly the same result. Twice lasting around five minutes before the hail stopped. I WAS CHANGING THE WEATHER. I used to get up in the morning and if their where clouds in the sky I used to sing "Here comes the sun" and not long after it would come out, I would lie in the shop doorway watching it rain at night and say quietly to myself "Stop the rain please" and then I would watch it stop minutes later or sometimes immediate. That is the way it was and had been for a long time, none coincidental. Prophecy or miraculous? I do not know what you would call it. It was one of the reasons why I was being watched and used. I knew that for sure. No it wasn't a form of mental illness or paranoia, religious belief and knowledge determined by life path.

I couldn't get to a T.V screen so I wasn't aware of anything happening in relation to the document or anything I had said, I didn't really make any friends but there where people I said hello to. As I have said Cathy was nice and I used to talk to her and had explained the situation to her surrounding who I was and what was going on, she listened politely and was curious and asked me a few questions when I had finished talking, I answered as best as I could, I think she understood by the time I had finished my explanation surrounding the different houses of truth and Nobility, linked to different names and blood lines, lineage etc. I explained to her that me working the miracle, where as it should have been a good thing was in fact a nightmare of exposure and it had destroyed my life. She was sympathetic and remained so. Whether she believed me or not I do not know. She was told the truth anyway. I continued sending out the document to thousands of people globally, universities and organisations and not just single names, churches and I even got the names of British police departments and sent it to them, I flooded Britain with it. It was going out well enough for me.

I used to spend some days sitting down by the River in the summer months a specific spot under an old oak tree on a long sloping bank, every day I would be there just sitting and passing time with nothing better to do other than to survive. Barrack Obama came to town on his campaign trail, set up camp right where I sat and gave a campaign speech. I put it down to a coincidence. Within the diary I was putting dates and places of my whereabouts as well as times. I was a world leader in covert circles don't forget. As I have said I put it down as a coincidence even though there where far batter places to give an open air speech in Portland. You can make your own mind up linked to my identity.

I was considering going home to Britain for some months now, but if I did decide on going back to Britain, how was I going to get there. I decided to give the Embassy another try and went on to the Internet to gain the address in Portland. I got it and it wasn't far to walk so I set off only to get there and find out the embassy had been closed in Portland. I didn't know what to do, phoning home and asking someone for money was out of the question no one I knew had enough money to spare. I had no choice I was going to have to "Fly a sign" This involved writing a sign and standing on a street corner holding it up asking for money. It was basically begging for money. The sign I had written wasn't a run of the mill begging for change sign, I went into detail stating I was the British Head of State and trying to gain airfare back to Britain and that I had worked miracles. It was around four foot by three foot in size and was difficult to hold so I stood it on the floor next to me. It didn't half raise some eyebrows. I had been down to the airport on the Tri Met train with a couple of dollars I had been given and had been told it was around $1,100 so I was going to be there for a while. I was day in day out after my time in the library and on the Internet at Daywatch. It was very slow, a relatively small city with an unbelievable sign, at least it was getting the message out. I was to have a serious problem one night whilst I was setting up to go to sleep in a shop doorway on the main road by the river. A red pick up truck had slowed as it drove past and winding down the window pointed out a gun at me and fired, the shot missed me ricocheting around the doorway. The van then sped off. Going to the police was a waste of time I was being taunted by them. One night around 3a.m a patrol car passed the doorway where I was sleeping and sounded the siren and then said over the loud speaker "Don't call us" and then laughed into the microphone like a demon. They had read it alright and all knew who I was. As I was walking along the Potomac River on the footpath there, a Catholic raised his arm as he walked towards me and made as if he had a gun and was shooting me. This is the way it was. I had declared war on the Catholic Church and sent it out to the Vatican and everyone else. I had no choice I was being held and used by them, yes I was aware George

W Bush was a Methodist but his administration wasn't and I would later change the document header to order the expulsion of the American diplomats over my treatment, I then sent it out to all American Embassies and the one in London. The security at the train terminal where I was flying the sign for airfare where taunting me as well, it was always third party taunts, as they where walking past talking to each other and no to restate it WASN'T PARANOIA on my part, they knew it was true alright and where worried, if I wasn't mentally ill they where in serious trouble. So therefore I had to be mentally ill, there confidence in it, the accusation, was plain to see in their actions and statements. From my knowledge I think it to be a standard accusation. Another night whilst sleeping I was awoken to a Bee Bee gun being fired into my face several times with the pellets landing all around my eyes and they ran off laughing, by the time I fully awoke they had gone. Yes the possibility of kids messing around was there, but the deal is I could have been blinded and the situation I was being held in was to blame. Taking someone's life and denying them their name because of complicity and perpetual ongoing game. The Catholic's wouldn't let up they even resorted to super gluing the computer room door lock to try to stop me writing the document, it was that futile. I would be writing the document and nearly finish my entry for the day only to watch it being wiped before my eyes, it was infuriating. Then I started to have all of my accounts closed down, luckily I had saved the document in another obscure account so could continue it, I must have opened at least forty new accounts over a month long period, I was being monitored and watched and again and again, I wasn't imagining it, they didn't mind me knowing what they where doing, they just didn't want anyone else knowing. They where trying to destroy evidence and stop me from logging it in the now journal. I was in no mans land between the ranks of the Windsor's and the Catholic Church. Protestants loyal to the Windsor's quite happy to allow it to go on and the Catholic's ripping me to pieces for my truth and miraculous knowledge. I had opened a bank account with my passport and over around four months of begging had amassed a princely sum of $100, There was no way I was going to make it, it would take years at this rate to save up the airfare to return. I bought a laptop from a local in a burger bar, I was having a coffee and he was selling one for $100. It meant I could really get some work on the document done and get it out. I amassed all of the email addresses of all of the politicians in Australia, Canada and Great Britain, hundreds of them. This lasted another couple of months and then I started to receive some very compromising pictures on my lap top and in fear of being set up, I sent them anonymously to the police from my lap top with the senders address and then worried about the possible set up I decided to destroy the lap top. All of the money wasted. I threw the lap top in the river at night. It was horrendous, the whole situation. Canada was looking good and wasn't that far away, just another state over. Washington State, I was considering it. I thought I would cross the border between posts to avoid any problems with customs at the border and a possible diplomatic incident. Had the truth been known it would have been a major diplomatic incident given who I was, as the police where involved, drugs and drug dealers had played a part as well. One of the things or points at which I decided to leave Portland came when I was stopped by a young student whilst walking around Portland centre one afternoon, he saw I was homeless and wanted to question a homeless person for his course studies at college, he politely asked me if he could interview me, I do not know if he knew who I was, but I agreed to the interview. We stopped by a small wall and leant against it. He started questioning me about life on the streets and how long had I been homeless and I told him what he wanted to know. He then asked me about drugs and alcohol, I said that a lot of the homeless did drink a lot. I also said that a lot of them where drug dealers, I had made a mistake and had meant to say drug addicts, there had been three fatal heroin overdoses in as many months on the homeless circuit there. He was a nice polite young man and I happily answered the rest of his questions and left. Less than twenty minutes later I was sitting at the galleria Tri Met train terminal in Portland and one of the homeless Catholic's passed me and looked across and said "Drug dealers?" With a questioning look on his face, a private and personal conversation had been somehow monitored and listened to. That was the level of the personal invasion of my life, the monitoring and perversion involved. Yes, they needed me to be mentally ill alright. Another incident took place on the Tri Met train in Portland, the Tri Met was a train that travelled through Portland to the airport and other destinations around the area, it was free to ride around the city centre and you only had to pay for longer journeys, I used to sit on it and ride up and down on the colder days in winter, it passed the time and was warm. On this particular day the market was on under the Burnside bridge, it was an open air market selling all kinds of Bric a Brac. The place and the train was packed with shoppers, I was sitting on the train and a there had been a problem with a full blooded Red Indian causing problems for passengers. The security had surrounded him and where watching but hadn't done anything about it. There was a blind man with a seeing eye dog or a guide dog as it is known in

Britain, the Red Indian in his thirties then tried to pick a fight with him. It was only then that the security escorted him off at the next station. I had recognised him from the homeless circuit. The next station was where the free rides ended so I had to get off as well. He punched the window nearly smashing it as he left the train and the security had "Bottled" it and not dealt with the situation and just let him walk off. I crossed the track and waited for the train to come back the other way for another free warm on the cold Saturday. The train pulled into the station and I boarded not even thinking about it. I stayed on until the Galleria area of Portland and got off. I walked across to the other side of the platform to again keep warm on the return journey until it was time to go to sleep. As I stood on the platform alone the Red Indian turned the corner and the train pulled into the station. My stomach turned, he was looking for trouble. I boarded the train and he followed me into the same carriage. It was empty apart from two other people. I sat down and he came and stood over me when there where empty seats everywhere, he had a long crucifix draped around his neck. He then pulled out a comb and started combing his long jet black hair whilst staring at me, I got up from my seat and started to walk to the other end of the carriage, as I started to walk away I could here him stamping his feet behind me and following me along the carriage. I sat down at the other end and he did the same thing standing over me, I again got up and left my seat moving down the other end of the train, being fully aware of the security cameras that where on all of the trains I knew it was being filmed. Apparently you get a prison term for fighting in Portland. Again he followed me stamping his feet and adopting a threatening posture when in my company, for the last time I would move. I got up and left my seat again, had the train been at a station I genuinely would have got off, but it wasn't it was in full flow. I was walking down the other end of the train past the two other passengers who where watching this and just before I sat down I slung my back pack on the seat and rounded on him without saying a word. I punched him four or five times and before he knew what was going on he was on the floor, one of the woman passengers was screaming into the panic speaker to the driver who stopped the train. As the train stopped in the station two more security guards stepped onto the train and arrested him saying "We have been looking for you" they where to late. The train driver asked me if I wanted the police calling and I said "No, what's the point" As I have said, luckily the entire incident is or was on camera so any action against me would have been futile, it was all on camera to be witnessed. I then had to face the thought of closing my eyes and going to sleep of a night in a shop doorway.

CHAPTER 13

Canada

Vancouver

I had decided to leave and it was nearly full on winter again and I was going farther North, without money or food, I would have to travel across an entire state and then slip into Canada unseen between posts and through the woods. I checked on the Internet to see where the homeless facilities where in Vancouver as a destination to head for. There was some listed so I knew I would be alright when I got there, one was the Union Gospel Mission on the Eastside of Downtown Vancouver. It would mean a few days without food and water but I would have to take the chance. I went to Daywatch and got some duck tape to make an airtight cover for my sleeping bag out of the tarpaulin I had. I fixed it up quite well just tight enough to house a sleeping bag securely. Then I made a cardboard sign to hold out on my journey. I handed the duck tape back in and asked someone to say goodbye to Cathy for me and left. I didn't say goodbye to anyone else. I had checked on the Internet for the right roads or highways to take and hitch on. It was a fair walk to the nearest highway ramp but I set off undaunted.

I got to the ramp in mid afternoon and waited for quite some time before I got a lift in a car going in my direction, it was only for seven miles but it was a start. I was dropped off by the driver at some place where he said I would get a lift through Washington towards Vancouver. It seemed desolate and I was right, I spent the rest of the day standing in the cold and had to go over to some shops when it had got dark to sleep in a doorway for the night. I got up the next morning early enough to avoid the shopkeepers and as I was walking back to the ramp I noticed a truck stop and decided to stand outside there. I spent most of the day there without any luck so I decided to move to another spot, it was freezing and I was waiting around for some time at that spot as well. I then decided to move up the ramp onto the highway itself and fly the sign for Vancouver, after several hours and in the dark, a camper van eventually stopped and said he could drop me at a truck stop just before Seattle in Washington State, I said "Great" and got in. Good enough some time later he dropped me off at the truck stop. It was a desolate small stop with trees all around it and I was at first unsure as to whether anyone actually stopped there. After some time cars and lorries started pulling in and I stood outside the toilets in the light flying my sign to Vancouver. I was there a few hours without any luck. Then I saw a man walking over to me from the other side of the truck stop, he approached me and said "I am going to Vancouver" He seemed shy and unsure as to whether to ask me if I wanted a lift. I said "Thanks that would be great" He had an old single decked bus converted to a camping van with a box trailer on the back housing a very small car. It was in the middle of the night and cold and I was glad to get in the warmth. It turned out that he was a Canadian and quite a nice guy. He asked me if I minded stopping off at the air museum before we crossed into Canada, he said that he would pay for a ticket for me to go in for the tour. I assured him that I didn't mind. We parked up the coach and bedded down for the night ready to go to the museum in the morning. Sure enough he paid for my ticket and a meal, I didn't have a penny to my name.

We did the tour and then where soon back on our way towards Canada. I explained to him my situation as regarding crossing the border and asked him if he could drop me near the woods and I would walk across the border. He said he didn't mind and we soon arrived near the border crossing, he decided to spend the night there and then took me out for a meal before crossing the border the next morning. He drove the small car he had hitched to the back of his trailer and we did a dry run to the border and along the road next to the crossing. We decided it would be best if I crossed at night and he kindly stayed all of the next day waiting for dark for me buying me breakfast. He got his maps out showing the Canadian side of the border and we discussed the best place to walk across through the woods and further onto the first road in Canada called "00 Road" Night fell and we again got into the small car and drove to the petrol station. He emerged from the petrol station and leaned across to me handing me some money saying "I hope this helps" I said thank you very much and as it was dark just put it straight into my pocket, I would later see that he had given me $100, what a nice guy. I can't even remember his name. We drove down the dimly lit back roads towards the border and he dropped me by the road we thought led straight to the woods and between border crossing, there where some farms and houses close to the border so I had to make sure I didn't just end up in someone's back garden and get arrested for trespassing. I said thank you to him, shook his hand and got out of the car and started walking down the dark road in what I hoped was the right direction. It was pitch black and I soon came across another road leading horizontal to the border, I had gone the right way. It was the last road in America, I walked along it looking for an opening to walk through the woods and after a few minutes I saw what looked like an overgrown path leading in the right direction, with no house or farms visibly near by I started to walk down it and was soon in dense undergrowth. Making enough noise as to be heard in a busy shipyard I trampled my way through the undergrowth and trees, eventually after around ten minutes of pitch dark wanderings I came into a small clearing, I was in the middle of the border, everywhere was silent and it was a bit eerie. I carried on walking and came to what seemed to be a thorn bush fence line it must have been right in the middle of the crossing, it was a nightmare to get through, I was cut to pieces with the sharp thorns and I would later get an infection in one of them and have to be treated. I eventually managed to get through the bushes and considered that I was on the Canadian side of the crossing. I then had to walk through another open clearing to get into Canada, this part was lighter and I ducked down whilst half running across the long open grass. I then reached another fence and tree line that was less dense on a raised hill, I climbed up and was happy to see a road, it was 00 Road and I was in Canada but still not out of the woods, I had to get some houses behind me so I wouldn't look like an illegal and get arrested by one of the constant patrol cars. I didn't walk down 00 Road and just went straight across towards what looked like a housing estate, it was much farther across if I could get there I would consider myself safe. I walked straight across through mud and grass and over fences towards the lights, after another ten minutes I was on the housing estate and just as I passed the first house in Canada a police patrol car came around the corner and drove towards me and straight past without slowing. I breathed a sigh of relief, I had made it. I now figured I had around a ten mile walk into Vancouver in the dead of night. I remembered my directions and headed for the road going straight into Vancouver. I walked for miles and miles along the road eventually hitting a small town and deciding to spend what was left of the night sleeping until the morning when I could change the money I had been given to Canadian dollars and get the bus or train the rest of the way into Vancouver. I awoke in the morning after sleeping near a bank and when it opened I went in and changed the money. I then headed for the bus terminal and was told it was a bus and train to Vancouver. I paid the money and waited and when the bus came I got on and then got onto the train into Vancouver. Once there I headed for the Union Gospel Mission and homeless facility. Once there I enquired about food and shelter and was given the information, they had mats on the floor and it opened at 9p.m, It was a first come first served basis but they where never full. No asked me too many questions and I got a meal and later on slept there for the night, it was warm and dry with a coffee in the morning. It was nearly Christmas again, I could have written a letter to the children at this point, but there was too much to say. I intended to get back to Great Britain somehow anyway. I would tell them about it in person.

Downtown Eastside was rough, drugs where rife on the streets, it seemed that of a night and indeed day most shop doorways had a crack addict in it smoking crack. It was really bad, the worst I had seen. There was a computer room at the Carnegie centre on East Hastings so I would be able to use the computer there as well as the library. I had again checked the rules in the main library in Vancouver and it was the same, one hour per day. Outside of the Carnegie centre on Hastings was a market place of drugs and drug dealers, you could get anything you wanted from morphine to heroin, crack and any tablets you wanted, that wasn't the surprising thing about the place, the surprising thing was that it was happening in full view of the police station only one hundred yards away and across the road. This was a rough area as I have said. The worst I had seen for drugs and dealers. Prostitution was rife on most street corners. I felt sorry for the woman, you could see they had been young and attractive when they got addicted to crack and then sold themselves on the streets to pay for their habit, it was horrible. All along East Hastings Road was a mass of homeless, drugs and alley ways with users, some addicts where on their hands and knees with pieces of wire going through the soil between the cracks in the pavement looking for small pieces of crack that someone may have dropped on the floor. You knew there wasn't any there but that was the level of the addiction. They got their benefit one day and it was gone that night on drugs, State benefit day was a hustling bustling day of excitement for them and the streets came alive on those days, some would actually be lying in the middle of the pavement on the main road in convulsions. I do not know what the police attitude was towards it, but it must have been lax. There where some homeless like me who didn't do drugs. But they seemed thin on the ground. It was accepted as normal or seemed to be by the police. It was no big deal. They could not have travelled much. There where around four shelters you could stay in the best of which was a fairly new building that was the Salvation Army shelter, they allowed you a thirty day stay out of every ninety. They had good facilities with a dining hall. I stayed at the Union Gospel mission at first because of the locality to the Carnegie centre and the computers, the library was farther away.

I was in Canada now and dealing with the Windsor's and cohorts again, impotent evidentially and their "Unknown forces" I walked into the Carnegie

Centre and immediately contacted the authorities and the immigration services to inform them that I was in Canada, I gave them a brief insight as to why I had had to leave America and explained that I had crossed the border between posts to avoid any incidents. I got no reply to my email. Over the next few days I contacted around thirteen offices, again by email and received no replies to any of them. I had informed them of my presence and could do no more. I was being monitored again, I was gaining hit's from private and personal emails I was sending out and being informed of it via third party information, an Irish catholic looking at me whilst I was walking past and making references directly to something I had just written. I was being viewed in my accounts, how they where doing it I am unaware. This is what they do, they where now uncaring as to my obvious knowledge of it with an attitude of "What are you going to do about it and what can you do?!" Well all I could do was to carry on with the document and carry on sending it out globally even if parts of it where wrong and the spelling was atrocious in my hasty necessity. I couldn't even contact the children, it was out of the question. I was very much being held and it was in fact a kidnapping in the public domain. Something I addressed in some depth within the document, I was going mad, not mentally mad although it would be understandable, I was furious, how dare they? It was like someone going through your underwear drawer, which wouldn't have surprised me if they had been. I had seen the capabilities and problems of some of these people and the last thing I wanted was my children on their minds given the obvious global capacity they had in the conspiracy.

Catching a vision was near impossible, I had never been able to do it and until recently didn't even realise I had been having them, I could have been having them all of my life without realising and may well have done. Even the vision of the woman winning the million I hadn't realised I had until I watched it in real time a week later on the T.V that was actually plugged in this time. So when I had the next one and realised I had just had a vision it was then that I started to realise who I truly was in all of it's madness. It was the most ridiculous event I could think of and so insignificant as to be mind boggling. I had been staying at The First United Church, the facility itself was the worst out of the lot, but it didn't have a curfew and you could leave the building at night and go for a coffee at the all night drop in centre so I stayed there on occasions. It was an old church as the name suggests, within the chapel they had erected around fifty bunk beds and the drug users and prostitutes used the place as a drop in unless otherwise outside smoking crack or plying their trade. It was rough basically, as rough as it gets. As I have said you got a lot more freedom of movement and latitude, in my situation it was welcome. Again as in the other shelters I had kept myself to myself to avoid any problems, it was best amongst the company although there where some nice people there obviously. Outside the main doors and down the concrete stairs from the shelter was a bus stop with a shelter over it. The homeless from the shelter used to sit in it drinking and smoking crack. One night at dusk I was standing in the lobby of the shelter overlooking the bus stop. I was just watching the rain that had just started dripping down the Perspex canopy of the bus shelter with three people sitting in it, I was just watching with nothing better to do and thinking about walking along the road for a cup of free coffee. I watched the bone dry road out the front start to get wet and change colour to the wet look that roads go after being dry. I decided that I wasn't going to go out and turned around to go into the dining hall and watch the film that was playing, I sat there for no longer than ten minutes and didn't fancy the film that was on and was going to go and get a coffee anyway. I got up and walked out of the dining hall and across the lobby and out through the front doors and down the steps towards the bus shelter and everything including the road was bone dry with the bus shelter empty. It hadn't been raining!? I knew then that I had just had some sort of vision, but what a ridiculous vision to have if you where going to have one at all. I went and had a cup of coffee lasting no more than twenty minutes at another facility just five minutes along the same road. I walked back to the Union Gospel Mission shelter and again was standing in the lobby and noticed that there where three people sitting in the bus shelter and within a minute it had started raining and drenching the road I then watched the drips dripping down the Perspex of the shelter in real time. So to ask me if I had visions, the answer would be yes but I do not know how or why and can not predetermine them.

The Catholic's where on form and I was beginning to wonder how they knew what I looked like since to my knowledge I had not been photographed. They had to have been watching me from that perspective as well for the recognition of me. Whilst sitting in another shelter, Tex an American druggie walked past me and looking at me said to his girlfriend "I'd cut his throat for the Pope" It is what you have to deal with, this was the Catholic's "Holier than thou" Being caught doing this to a man who they knew to have worked miracles, in the safety and belief of the safety of an unstable accusation of mental illness. I feared for the safety of my children but didn't mention it in the document. The severity of the situation was brought to light by a

Protestant woman who walked past me one night whilst I was having a walk to get away from the shelter and madness there. She was English or certainly spoke with an English accent and was walking with I assume her husband or boyfriend. I was walking slow and taking in the shop windows. She and her man walked directly towards me and as I approached her and him she looked directly at me and said "They are going to kill you for this" I know they where Protestants. But the interesting thing is, they didn't offer any help or ask me if I was o.k, I was defending them by way of evidential exposure without any choice in the matter because of how heinous the problem is and was. Trapped between the ranks and isolated in Prophecy and Nobility with nowhere to turn being berated by my own people and faith. They had to have been loyalists loyal to the Windsor's. A Protestant in ignorance of this, on enlightenment would be furious and justifiably so. That was there attitude, dragged into the gutter after working miracles, having my children threatened. Being mentally raped and left for dead. All because my life interfered with the Windsor conspiracy of silence and accusing cover up, together with the fact that they where impotent evidentially and conspiratorial with the Catholic Church. I,e "We cant prove it and don't have the evidence to prove and stop it so who the hell do you think you are nutter!?" They where not the Heads of State with me around, that was the problem, my existence reality and truth was their downfall if the truth was known and out "When all things where naked and open". A miracle takes the throne, especially when you are a Protestant and your lineage goes back before the tenth century Britain. Even more so when it is linked to a crime against the people and State, as Emma Bunton said, it should have stopped their sick game, but because they where the criminals it didn't.

I was planning to leave for some time but couldn't figure out an angle to get home and hit on a long shot, I would try to work my passage on a cargo ship, I had taken the relevant courses when I was working on the oil rigs but all of my certification had been stolen in Los Angeles with everything else, I was even on the wrong side of the coast so it really was a long shot. I still had not heard anything from immigration even though I had sent them over twenty emails at this point, stating situation and identity. I walked along to a local seaman's mission and spoke to the Chaplain there, he was not a Catholic but I am unsure as to his belief structure. He invited me into his office and I told him in detail of my situation inclusive of miracles and asked him if he knew of anyone I could approach with a view to working my passage back to Britain. He confirmed my thoughts stating I was on the wrong side of the coast for Atlantic shipping. He was actually quite a nice man, I said thank you anyway and left. My last hope now was the British Embassy in Vancouver so I got the address from the Internet and hoped it was still there. It wasn't far and I walked there. When I went in I told the woman at the desk of my situation and was treated with an uncaring attitude and stonewalled. I lost my temper, it was disgraceful. I had spoken to one of the Canadian homeless people, who was ex army and he told me of an incident in Vietnam whereby a British citizen was as much as left for dead on the streets by them, a man who was in severe difficulty getting home. He also said most countries provided at least one free flight for genuine hardship as Canada did, apart from Britain, they didn't want to know. I let my feelings be known and stated that the Windsor's where going to hang for this. They really do not care and to get them to act on anything is problematic to say the least. They represent the Windsor's and higher ranks in the structure and will not be bothered by anything or anyone unless it is news worthy and have to be seen to be doing something. They have nice holidays at those Embassies and Consulates. That is all they are good for, I also asked her if there was a man there and she stated there wasn't. I then decided to go and see if I was entitled to any benefit being a British citizen in British Columbia given it was a monarchist domain but was refused after a wasted two days of going around offices and filling in forms. I really was stranded and now was reluctant to even make a phone call to anyone for fear of their safety, such was the monitoring and just to elaborate, this wasn't any form of watchful protection either. It was perverted invasion and very sinister at best, I was getting constant in your ear hits from private emails I was sending out, I was having them or exerts from them played back to me and I wasn't imagining it either.

I had stopped using the Carnegie centre as much. I thought the security at the terminals there where compromised and I was right, I assumed that the security system at the library terminals would be better, I was wrong. I spent a lot of time in the library. The Olympics where coming up and I had received a letter or email from a local woman interested in corresponding which was unusual, it was one of the very few in nearly seven years. I immediately panicked and wasn't sure as to what to do, I was worried for her safety, if they where watching me they where also watching people in my company. It was a dilemma. She wanted to meet for coffee and a chat. I sent her an email back reluctantly agreeing against my better judgement and to be honest with you in the situation I was in, I was unfair. I really didn't think it safe for her to be in my company. We arranged to meet in the main library and would contact each other by email when we where both there, I got there at the relevant time and emailed her the number of my computer terminal. I waited for her and she turned up a few minutes later. She was attractive and nice, a Canadian, whether she knew who I was or not I am uncertain but think she may have done. We spoke of the coming winter Olympics in Vancouver which where months away and she wasn't to keen on them saying she thought they where a waste of money. She then asked me if I wanted to go for a coffee and I said I didn't have any money and she offered to pay. We left the library and went across the road and she bought me a coffee. We talked about this and that and nothing in particular, she was nice and quite shy. She lived in a flat alone and said it was cold. It was just a basic conversation. We finished our coffee and it was getting late and she said she had to go, remembering the possible danger I offered to walk her to the train station and put her on the train back to her home, she agreed and we walked to the station and she gave me a hug before she left and got on the train. The next day I sent her an email thanking her for the coffee and the chat. Within the email that was fairly long as I went into an explanation as to why I thought the Olympics where a good thing as it brought in revenue that I thought would out way the expense. I then stated in the email that we would be looking back in a couple of years saying "Hey remember Vancouver 2010" I sent the email to her and thought no more of it, yet aware of the monitoring I was under, albeit their was obviously nothing I could do about it, I had changed passwords in my accounts several times and it had made no difference. I am not really computer literate and have not got a clue how it was being done I only know it was. A good few months later I was watching an apocalyptic disaster film called 2012 when my ears pricked up, had I just heard that right? In one of the scenes, the actors where on one of the ships ready to depart, one actor said to another, it was completely out of context from the script. He said "Remember Vancouver 2010" Now that was a direct hit lifted from a private email I had sent, the document and me where that live and present. The film came out very soon after they had lifted it from me and I wasn't imagining it either. They are the kind of hits you are getting. That is the kind of people involved in it, the way the word spreads and messages passed within the organisation. Within the document I had some emails I had sent as evidence that I copied and placed within the document to prove it along with the monitoring to belay any accusations of paranoia. In short it couldn't be denied. I had the dated evidence and emails along with a copy I had taken of someone else being in my email account whilst I was in another. It was undeniable. I was the entertainment industries Cesar remember and an historic man, I wasn't a player in their game I wasn't a gamed creation or actor, I was real. I was born famous. I was famous enough to be believed, but if I was believed the Windsor's where finished and that is what they didn't want, the Windsor's couldn't stop their sick perverted game without any evidence. I was being held and used whilst being accused of insanity for complaining. The total recognition came when I was squatting outside the library smoking a cigarette, a man walked past me and no one else was in the immediate vicinity, he had a quick look around and then looking at me he coughed twice, under each cough was a word, the first word was "Your" and the second word was "Cesar" He had basically coughed to cover up he was informing me I was Cesar. It was as if that his or their knowledge of my historical identity made all of this acceptable.

I cant remember whether Tony Blair turned up in

Vancouver talking about God and religion before or after the Olympics but no, I do not believe it was coincidental to my being there, though there is always the possibility, if it wasn't I could have got a restraining order on him?

The miraculous events had subsided so I thought and I spent most days now in the library updating the document and when my hour was up I would walk around looking for a terminal with some time left on it, I usually found one. One day I remember just browsing the Internet reading the news and spent some time reading an article about a massive Tsunami in Japan with thousands of dead as it had washed right across the country, luckily I then updated the document and made reference to it and what I had just read. I wasn't speaking to anyone now at all, I had or was having problems with a couple of local druggies, who had taken a dislike to my silence probably and thought I was an easy mark in the situation I was in, I was also aware that they all knew who I was. There was a druggie gang culture their and you had to be careful. I witnessed one fight break out and a whole host of the homeless druggies from the same gang had no hesitation in jumping in and all over the poor man who was alone. It was that base and unacceptable, the place was out of control and in sight of the police station. They had obviously come to accept it as normal. Though so bad was the drug problem of using and dealing across from the police station, I had considered the possibility of police corruption and involvement. It was that bad and open. I also had a problem with my tooth that I needed dealing with and had to go to a free clinic manned by volunteers along East Hastings Road to get two teeth pulled. I walked in, got an injection and had the two teeth pulled and the gums stitched back up. I spent the next month or so pulling out bits of broken teeth that where working their way out of my gums, I was in quite some discomfort whilst removing the broken shards of teeth. This was my life, held and used as well as accused. All for doing the right thing in the face of the unacceptable having my own people walking past telling me I was going to be killed for not accepting it and the perversion my children had been under albeit unknown to them. How did I know that they wouldn't be approached by one of the voyeur's watching? Lets face it the entertainment industry is full of unsavoury characters isn't it! Who decides who watches? Who gives the permission? The Catholic's all watch. It was sick.

I had been contacting the police with the document for months, I had gained numerous email addresses of departments and various divisions all of which I placed within the document and sent it out to all of them with then addresses of the White House and the Vatican in the same address bar so they could all see who was reading it. I eventually got a response from S.O.C.A, Serious organised crime or something. It was a sarcastic email entitled "Dear madam" I was furious, this was serious and they where now treasonous in visibility and in the face of offered evidence undeniable. I sent him a very nasty email back saying that I was going to return to Britain at some point and that I was going to pay him a visit and since I had a licence I was in my rights to kill him for putting my life in danger by way of false accusation of mental illness. Legally and in truth I was right, it was in the face of evidence to prove a conspiracy. In reality, they had the ball and the media as well as the mental health teams on their side. As well as a complicit organisation that in no way would admit to doing this for fear of war. I was lost at the very least I thought that once it got into court it would be researched and seen for what it was. The term "Let right be done" is supposed to be the bedrock of the British establishment and judicial system. Yes I was wrong in doing it but I was under psychological torture. I knew they now had the ball and in their domain and an illegal family in the palace I was on the wrong side of their law. They could arrest me. If it went to court I could blow them to pieces with the evidence of miracles undeniable. The document would be within the judicial system and my job would be finished. I would have proved it and got my name linked to my historical identity. I then got a response from an officer in Britain, I think called Donna, who stated that she wanted to know my whereabouts and I immediately responded with an email telling her not only my location but the terminal number I was at and the times I visited the library. I was very frank surrounding treason rape and paedophilia all of which I addressed within the document. I explained if the truth came out about this conspiracy involving the Catholic Church they could very well hang for all of the aforementioned. I had all of the evidence. After I sent the email I heard nothing more from her. Months had passed as well as another Christmas alone without my children and no hope of contact for fear of their safety. I was still having trouble with a few of the local druggies at The First United Church so I decided to move to another shelter. This one I had been unaware of until recently. It was another Catholic based charity. As serious as it was anyway, given the problems I was having with the druggies I was also aware of the danger I was in given who I was, so I made a last ditched attempt at contacting the Consulate Embassy and I phoned up from the second older Salvation Army shelter near to Hastings. It was Catholic's who where running the place and as I spoke they where listening as they usually do. I spoke for a minute or two surrounding the situation and a woman I think called Gail Blair put the phone down on me on realising who I was. I am unaware if Gail Blair is any relation to Tony Blair but it wouldn't surprise me. They will not give anyone assistance. Which begs the question as to why they are there in the first place?

I booked in to another catholic shelter near the main library after checking to see if there where any beds. The first time you stayed there you got three months grace. There was no food but they handed out tokens in the morning for McDonald's and you could get food from there aside from the other free meal services so it wasn't too bad. The dorms where only half full as well which was another bonus, I do not know why others didn't stay there as well. Maybe because it was Catholic, I had no intention of discussing anything with anyone there so felt o.k. They also had two computer terminals which was handy for me. You had to be out by 7a.m and couldn't come back until 4:30p.m so you where out for the day come rain or shine. I carried on visiting the library for the next month or so and used the terminal in the shelter of a night. Then one night at around 1a.m in the morning I was awoken to a light shining in my eyes with two police officers standing there and another man. The other man asked me to identify myself and told me he was from the immigration services. I was taken out of the dorm and into the T.V room which was empty, he questioned me as to my legality and I told him what had happened and why I was there, I also told him how many times I had tried to and actually contacted the immigration services in Canada and he said nothing. He asked me if I wanted to pursue a stay in Canada or if I was going to accept deportation, as I was planning to go home I said I would accept deportation. With that he gave a signal to the two officers to go back into the dorm and get the rest of my belongings and as they disappeared out of the door towards the dorm he jumped up and sat on the table next to me, he was very close to me and almost whispered into my ear "You are not going to fight us are you?" At that point I was aware he knew who I was and knew my identity, I also believe he was another Catholic and it was in reference to that, that he spoke. After I had said "What?!" In a disbelieving tone and gave him an angry look at what he had just said he quickly retreated back over to the other chair before the two police officers came back into the room. I was then arrested, cuffed and taken down to a waiting van with a cell in the back and loaded in. We then went to a holding cell to be processed. I stayed in there for around half an hour and was eventually processed and on processing another van came and I was taken to the airport holding cell in Vancouver. I was told that there would be a hearing before I was to be deported. I think it may have been a weekend and I stayed there until the Monday. It was a basic room with three or four other rooms off it with beds in and there was a shower room as well. There where two other people in there and we where asked what we wanted to eat at various times and they went out to a takeaway for it. It was o.k and comfortable with a T.V and board games in there. Monday came and again the van was there, we where handcuffed and taken out to the van and then driven on to the immigration courts in Vancouver. I was photographed and fingerprinted and then allowed to phone my court appointed solicitor. All this time we where waiting in a holding cell and eventually our solicitors turned up and my turn came and when I went in I went through the now infuriating task of explaining the situation and what was going on, he listened and said the hearing was scheduled for a few days time. He then left and after some more time I was called to speak to another solicitor and had to go through the whole thing again. The day ended and we where taken back to the holding tank at the airport and after a couple of days we where driven back to Vancouver for our court hearing. I sat in the holding tank until my appearance. We where again cuffed and shackled and led out to the lift and up to the court room in the building, I walked in to see my solicitor to my left and two what I would think where prosecutors on my right who where both men. I walked over and sat next to him and then a minute or so later the judge walked in and sat down, the hearing was opened and the prosecutor spoke first and started lying through his teeth saying I had made no attempt to contact the immigration since I had been in Canada, I wasn't arguing with anyone about it, I was eventually returning to Britain, what was the problem? He then entered into a vague discussion with the judge about something and the judge dismissed him saying I do not see any problem with it. She was referring to the document and so was he, he was seemingly getting quite annoyed and she dismissed him again. It must have been eating them alive, a Protestant commoner with noble lineage going back over a thousand years catching the Catholic Church out with a miracle. They all gave the impression of being British in origin apart from my solicitor who I think was Jewish and not of British origin. I was then told that I was being expelled from Canada and that I could not return there for one year after which time I could. I was happy with that. I then left and was taken back to the airport. I was scheduled for departure the following Tuesday I think it was. The next day I was thinking we would just be staying in the holding tank at the airport until someone came in and we where told we where going back to Vancouver. We where again shackled and cuffed and taken back, after some time in the cell there I was called in for an interview with the immigration officer who was to escort me from Canadian soil. She wanted to see if I was mentally stable and to make sure I was going to go off my head on the flight. I was furious but didn't show it. They where still trying to get away with the accusation. She left after around twenty minutes satisfied that I was stable. I was then taken back into the holding cell and after a few minutes I was again called out to the interview room. When I walked in there where two men in there who identified themselves as police officers. Again they where both British in origin, one of them placed a tape recorder on the desk in front of me switching it on and sat back in his chair. They where both very nervous and I was thinking that this didn't look very legal as the judge had already made a ruling on me and the deportation as well as the document. They started to question me about the Embassy and my visit there. They tried to make it look as if I had just attacked two little old ladies in hair nets. When in fact all I did was to voice my serious concern over the issue surrounding treason and my sacrifice to the Catholic's, as it was becoming apparent this was. I then explained the situation surrounding my exit from American soil into Canada telling them of the police involvement and the Catholic backed conspiracy. He then told me to write a book about it, now in real terms and in light of evidence and truth he was or had actually just tried to pervert the course of justice by way of ignoring a crime and he stated it on tape. The interview went to and fro with one of the officers "Lolling" all over the table as I was talking, then one of the officers became quite friendly with me saying and stating on tape that he had a brother in law who was paranoid and he said to me that he didn't think I was paranoid in any way as he could recognise the symptoms, again he stated all of this on tape. The meeting then ended and nothing more was said and they left. We where kept in the cells for the rest of the day and then I was again called out and shackled and hand cuffed and taken to the van. This time I wasn't driven to the airport, I was driven to a local prison and processed to be put in circulation. No one had told me what was going on or how long I would be there. It was obviously Monarchist based. I was processed and given a box with the words EVIL written on it and had to parade around with it. I looked around the other boxes of the prisoners and I was the only one with it written on. Whether it was a coincidence I am unaware but wouldn't be surprised if it wasn't. I was then allocated a cell and spent two nights there wondering what was going on unable to gain any information from the guards. After the two days I was called to the desk to be processed for leaving. The van was there again and I was driven to the airport holding tank. I was told that I would have time for a shave and a shower. After I showered and dressed the woman who had interviewed me about my sanity turned up with an Irish Catholic in tow, they where pleasant enough and stood in the cells waiting for one of the guards to come in to give me my belongings. As he did he walked towards me and reached out with my things to me but stretched out as far as he could and handed them to me, I was being treated as if I was a raving lunatic and he was terrified of going near me. We left the centre and this time I was just hand cuffed, we walked through some corridors and out onto a small loading bay where the woman handed me a pack of twenty cigarettes. It was good of her and I thanked her, I had asked her for a cigarette at the interview and she had bought me twenty for the trip. The Irish Catholic didn't say to words to me the whole journey. I am unsure as to what religion she was.

I had two cigarettes and was then walked through to the terminal and she asked me if I wanted a jumper to cover the handcuffs whilst I walked through and I said no let them all see, anyone who knew who I was that is. I was being treated like a petty criminal. We boarded the plane and I asked if she was going to "uncuff" me during the flight and mentioned that take off and landing was the most dangerous part of the flight. She said "We'll see" We boarded the plane and sat at the back I was ushered into a window seat and as the plane took off I offered her my wrists across the seat and good enough she took the cuffs off. The flight was basic enough and we soon landed in London.

CHAPTER 14

London England

Hillingdon

Once in London we disembarked and walked straight through the customs and I was ushered over to another exit at the side. There where two men and one woman wearing civvies waiting at the checkout. The woman who had escorted me from Canada handed one of the men my back pack and turned to me and said goodbye, they hadn't even told me what was waiting for me in London. I was arrested and not told of the charges and taken out of the airport, they where police and I later wondered whether they where Royal protection squad but was never told. I was then ushered into the back of a police van and taken to the airport police station and held in a cell. They still would not tell me the charges. The desk sergeant took my details and I was searched. They took all of the details of the email accounts with the document in and confiscated them. I had a small note book with all of the account details in. I told him to go into one of the accounts and read the document as long as it was. I was arrested but not charged with anything at this point and had questioned as to why but was told "Not yet" by one of the officers in plain clothes. They then began to talk to me. We stepped outside and had a cigarette, they where all smoking mine as it happens. They asked me what was going on and I went into the long explanation surrounding nobility and houses and the Catholic Church and the Protestant Faith. The gross perversion and kidnapping involved in this sick scenario. I went into some depth surrounding "The Game" They where playing with me and who I was, miracles inclusive. I looked across at the woman at this point and she understood every word I was saying to her, it wasn't hard to understand, very simple, it was written all over her face in shock and horror yet they all feigned ignorance of understanding. I explained that in this situation they where upholding the Windsor's and not the law and by my miraculous deed and definition, truth and lineage, they where outranked. I told them I had historical placement as well as a right to justice however far it went. They became very friendly and I went back to my cell and asked to phone a solicitor. I was given the number of a solicitor some time later and thinking it was going to end up in court I didn't feel worried at all, at least I would gain representation and the document and evidence would then be in the judicial system for everyone to see and read. No, I wasn't worried. I was called out to speak to my appointed solicitor and picked up the phone. He asked me if I had been charged and I said "No" He told me not to speak to them at all but that was obviously to late, he told me not to say anything in the station at all as it was monitored, he also told me not to say to much on the phone as they where probably tapped, this was a solicitor with knowledge. I expected him to turn up later as he said. I went back to my cell. A few minutes later the cell door opened and I was called out, they said there where some people who wanted to speak to me. I was ushered into a side room in the station and was confronted by four people. They informed me they where from the mental health and wanted to speak to me, they had phoned up the shrinks. I had shown no signs of anything. It is standard procedure in cases like this, I knew that much. An accusation of mental illness circumnavigates the court room and you never get representation. You do not even get a solicitor with any power. You are very much in no mans land at the mercy of a psychological book worm, some of them, as Dr Parhee was, are very power hungry and will not listen to a word they are being told such is there arrogance. I really was devastated when I saw who they actually where, not one of them was English or Protestant. Explaining to them about nobility, truth and houses was going to be impossible. I was right, one of them was a Czech, one of them was an Indian one of them was an African and one of them was another Eastern European. I had no chance. I was questioned and refused to answer stating they where not even in my belief structure. It wasn't a racist statement it was just the way it was. I didn't even have representation or an ear of one of my own people such was the situation. They didn't have a clue surrounding nobility and truth along with justice. I said as little as I could. The last question came from the African in broken English, he couldn't even speak the language and was sitting in judgement on me, there where lots of sympathetic smiles which really bugged me. He turned to me and swinging backwards on his chair for his "Moment" in front of the other psychologists and sounding very cool he said "If you had a gun" I cut him short and said "Hang on a minute I am not going through this any more" and then stated their differing ethnicity's to mine and the situation they where not qualified by definition of birth or knowledge to sit in judgement on me and certainly where not well enough informed. It was like educating the blissfully ignorant every time I had to explain it to them. The meeting ended with more feigned and sympathetic smiles. I walked out of the room in disarray and into the three officers who asked what had happened and I told them they where not even

British, how the hell could they understand nobility being from a foreign background? The officers looked sympathetic and I was then led to the desk to be charged. I was to be charged on a "Fixated threat" and a "Threat to kill" I was told I was being bailed until some months later. I was then placed back into my cell not feeling too bad at least it would be in court. I was jet lagged and I slept for some time, how long I do not know but had given food at some point. Then the cell door opened and one of the plain clothed officers looked in and basically said "I am going now, nice to meet you but you are a nutter!" and closed the door and left, I was stupid to trust them or expect any justice. Mr nice guy copper wasn't at all. I was still being held after being charged and bailed, some time after this the cell door opened and a uniformed officer was standing there and escorted me out. He said come with me and there was an ambulance waiting outside. I got in without complaint or knowing what was going on. I was then driven to and admitted to Hillingdon mental health unit. I had been sectioned again. I got onto the ward and was gain dismayed to see that not one of the staff was of my ethnicity or indigenous to my own country and faith. Now, again, I am not a racist but this was serious, I was being stonewalled and thrown to the wolves by my own people, purely for telling the truth about the unacceptable. To explain to these people about justice and treason, who where in total subservience to a crown they knew nothing about in a foreign country to their own was impossible. To expect any help was ludicrous. I was on a lock down ward and couldn't leave. I was shown my room and slept there for the rest of the night. The next day I woke up and tried to find out how long I was going to be there. I was not getting any information but was told there was a meeting arranged for tomorrow with a ward psychologist or psychiatrist I can not remember which. The head Honcho of the wards basically. I noticed that there where two computer terminals on the ward, but all of my passwords and access codes had been confiscated or so I thought, I thought they had the full document and all of the accounts, until I checked my wallet that is. I found a small piece of paper with a few passwords and account names in it. I held my breath and logged on to the terminal and tried the first name and password. It had been closed. I sighed and then tried another with the same result. They had closed my accounts. I then tried the last one and it opened. The document with evidence was safe and I could still work with it. I thought I had lost all of the evidence to the police who had in turn closed all the accounts and destroyed the document, or so they thought, so had I for a moment. I quickly opened up another account and transferred the document over and closed it again, I wasn't going to do any work on it in the hospital but was still going to keep a small diary of these events for the purposes of history, I was determined that this was coming out. I wasn't going to be labelled some historical nut case for the benefit of the evidentially impotent Windsor's and their cohorts. But moreover it was important for my children.

The day of the meeting came and I was called in to a room and was faced by none English people, the woman was a Pakistani in origin and another one was African, I am talking about first generation immigrant English here, not indigenous, it wasn't their skin colour it was their knowledge that was the problem or to be more accurate, their ignorance and lack of knowledge surrounding justice and legality of perversion together with house and name. I had and was having my house ransacked by the Catholic's with loyal Protestant complicit "Tough" laughter. There wasn't any justice and to talk to them was futile. Then I looked farther across the room and there seemed to be an English man sitting there with a laptop on his knee preparing to take notes of the meeting. I was then questioned by one of the two Pakistani women. I think the underling, probably practising in front of her tutor. I explained everything yet again to her and them. I finished and she seemed satisfied and then the chairwoman of the meeting in the corner piped up and looking at a medical chart on her knee she said "When you where in Clatterbridge you where on" She then reeled off the name of some drug or other , I wasn't paying much attention but my ears pricked up when she said that I said "What could you repeat that please?" She did and I then informed her that I had not been on any drugs in Clatterbridge at all and was discharged without taking them. Dr Parhee had falsified medical records of drug administration and it couldn't have been an accident. I wasn't going to let it go and said "What is going on here? I have never been on drugs in a hospital!" She then became very defencive and moved the document off her knee and out of sight. The last thing you can do in front of these people is lose your temper and you do not want to get into an argument with them, they hold keys over your head and have an awful lot of power over you, once they get a grip of you, you are in trouble if you are telling the truth, silence is the best option. I had to let it go. Dr Parhee had committed a crime and was now part of the conspiracy. Why she had done it I do not know. I left the meeting just after that point seriously worried about what I was going to do. Me and my children where being watched in our own homes and I was having my phones tapped. Now, how hard is that to understand!? Also given the horrendous episodes of the phone tapping scandals where just about to come out it wasn't that unbelievable. "Oh and by the way, they witnessed me working a miracle as well, crapped in their pants and tried to cover it all up" Not hard to believe is it?

The staff on the ward where worse than incompetent and it obviously went to the top when the jobs where being handed out, a couple of them could only just about string a sentence together in English and obviously where not qualified to do the job or if they where something was seriously wrong. I stood in a queue one night for a headache tablet for over an hour behind four people waiting for two tablets each and they couldn't read the medication chart, one man was asking why his medication had been changed to this particular tablet and was brushed off and dismissed, he had been given and was going to take the wrong medication. There where a couple of men with serious problems and it was hard work. It was an all male dorm or ward. The next day I tried to gain more information and was told that I was due for another meeting in a couple of days. I wasn't showing any signs of anything, OBVIOUSLY. So was probably under observation in their incompetence. They take notes and fill in forms, though I doubt they where done properly. After a few days I received a phone call and was asked to go to the office. It was my daughter on the phone, someone had got in touch with my aunt and next of kin and they had notified my daughter on a social networking site. I was overjoyed, she started crying and I was nearly crying myself, I hushed her and started talking to her. I had missed so much of her life, seven years of being away without contact. After a few minutes the years rolled away and we where talking as if no time had passed at all, it was lovely, I felt a warmth I had not felt for quite some time. I enquired about Emily and Jack and she said they where fine and Jack was at university. I had missed so much and missed them so much it was hard for me. We arranged more contact the next day and finished the conversation. I was now in contact with someone who I loved and knew loved me, it cheered me up no end.

It must have been the next day whilst sitting in the T.V lounge watching T.V. A news report came on, there had just been an earthquake in Japan and the ensuing Tsunami had killed around 27,000 people. I was shocked and a little upset. What was going on? I had already seen this! This had already happened months ago, I had seen it in Vancouver, read about it! I watched it unfolding on the news and didn't know what the hell to do. I didn't discuss it with anyone. I had put it in the document even though it was yet to happen. If nothing else it was a dated and recorded entry of proof that I wasn't making it up or imagining it. I had sent the entry out as well so couldn't be accused of altering it after the fact. It was now undeniable I was having visions of things to come. But again I could still not pin them down or understand when it was happening. I only ever realised after the fact. But this was documented. It wasn't or hadn't been a hallucination either and I couldn't be accused of having them. I had caught one by accident in evidence and chronological dated and documented reference.

The next meeting was scheduled for the afternoon and I waited around, when the time eventually arrived I was called in to the same room and another set of people where in there and I had to go through the whole rigmarole again. Again it was a Pakistani woman only a little younger, around thirty or so. I explained myself and then had a change of tack and started to question her politely about belief structure and faith. She then asked me about mine and I explained to her my beliefs and values. She seemed to understand and the meeting ended. The next day I was told that I was no longer on lockdown and could go out. I needed to sign on the dole to get some money sorted out so I made an appointment at the job centre and when the time arrived I walked into Hillingdon Town centre and filled out the relevant forms. It felt good to be out in the fresh air and no mention of me taking any drugs had been made. So it wasn't looking to bad although I was still locked up. They told me at the job centre that it would take up to six weeks and I could apply for a crisis loan, something I hadn't done as yet as I didn't need any money for anything since I was still being held in the hospital. I was then called into the office again and asked where I wanted to go and I didn't understand the question, they said I was due to be released soon and "Where did I want to go?" I could go anywhere and wasn't sure where to go. I said I would have a think about it and get back to them. The mental health services have a duty of care and can't put someone out onto the street. They have to make sure you are placed as you are their responsibility. So I thought about it for the rest of the day and thinking I could go anywhere I walked back into the office and said "I would like to live in Cumbria" They said o.k. I was to have another meeting in a couple of days on the Friday when I was to be discharged. I had no money to travel or go anywhere. I addressed the situation with one of the staff members and spent quite some time trying to get through to her, she couldn't understand English very well. I eventually got it across to her and she started making phone calls looking for a homeless shelter or a hostel in Windermere in the Lake District. I left her to it and went back into the T.V lounge. The next day was Thursday and she came into the T.V room and said she had some phone numbers for me to phone when I got to Windermere in Cumbria. She gave me the numbers and left. I still had no money. The next day I was again called into the office and the woman asked me to come with her, she took me to a small room and sat me down and pulled out a cash box and counted out around £85 and said that was the train fare to Windermere and then gave me some money to travel across London to the train station. She assured me that I would have a place to stay when I got there. All I would have to do was make a phone call. I left the room and was then called in to my discharge meeting. After a few minutes I left and had been discharged with nothing being done, nothing being stated a s to my mental health or lack of it. I was just discharged, the whole thing had been a waste of time and I was left very curious as to what was going on. I was still under police bail but had already decided that I wasn't going to turn up for court it would be a waste of time. I would let the warrant run. I sent the police an email informing them of my none intention to turn up at the appointed court date and left it at that.

CHAPTER 15

Cumbria England

I walked to the nearest tube station in Hillingdon and had decided that I was not going to get the train to Cumbria but was going to get the National coach service as it would be cheaper and I could save some money. So I boarded the train and went to the nearest coach terminal. I walked up to the checking counter and asked for a ticket to Windermere in Cumbria and the woman looked at me and said "Where?" I said again "Windermere in Cumbria" She was foreign and said "There is no such place" and dismissed me for the next customer, I went to another window and asked the same question and was told that all of the buses to the Lake District went from London Victoria. I asked her to book me a ticket and she said there wasn't one going until tomorrow. I asked her to book it anyway and then travelled across London with my ticket to Victoria coach station. I went for a drink of coke in the nearest pub and had a walk around the local area having a glass of coke here and there. I slept in the coach station for the rest of the night. The next morning I still had a few hours to wait and I was walking along the road near the station passing some time when a woman walking towards me looked at me directly into my face and talking to me said "Are you scared yet?" She was a Latino in appearance and I dismissed it as a coincidence but put it in for the "Maybe" aspect of it. I was this famous amongst them. It was and still is a form of terrorism and psychological torture that they feel safe in operating to because of how closed the

Catholic Church and it's game is.

I boarded the coach and set off to Windermere. It was late evening when we got there and the first thing I did was look for a phone box and called one of the three numbers I had been given, it wasn't a shelter and I was told that there where not any shelters in Windermere. I phoned up the other two numbers with the same result. I was stuck and I didn't even have a sleeping bag. I decided to try and see if I had any better look in Kendal and walked to the train station and boarded a train to Kendal. I was there in a few minutes. It was late and I was looking for somewhere to stay, I tried the local Y.M.C.A without any luck it was to expensive and I ended up standing and walking around all night. There was a McDonald's burger bar that was to open at 6a.m or so I was told I waited nearby and good enough at 6a.m it opened and I walked in and ordered a coffee and sat down waiting for things to open. After a few minutes another man walked in and sat down opposite to me. I just said to him "Do you know of anywhere where the homeless can go to get food and shelter here?" He said that he did and introduced himself as Craig. I was in luck. It was to open later and was called The Manna. He said that he would take me there. He was a nice guy I am unaware of his religion. We stayed there for an hour or so and a couple of other people came in, another one was homeless as well so I was on the right track and would maybe get some sort of sleeping bag from the place called Manna. We arrived at The Manna and it wasn't far away and they had or where serving food later on so I could get fed. I asked them for a sleeping bag after explaining my situation and luckily enough they had an old one. I would be on the streets though as there where no shelters available, I was told that Lancaster would probably be the nearest, a train journey away and I didn't have the money. The other homeless guy was sleeping in a shed nearby. The job centre wasn't open until Monday and I couldn't get a crisis loan until then. So I was stuck until Monday, I spent the night in an alley way and again visited the McDonald's early in the morning and good enough Craig was in there again, so at least I had someone to talk to, he was very helpful which was nice. I hadn't told them anything of my identity and was unaware as to whether they knew though I do not think they did. As soon as the job centre was open I went in and informed them of my change of location. I filled out the relevant forms and signed on. I then went to a phone around the corner and applied for a crisis loan. It wouldn't be much, I phoned up and got one, I can't remember how much it was, twenty pounds or something. It wasn't enough to leave and I was thinking about living there for a while. The Manna was open daily and it had a phone you could use. I was just glad to be back in Britain and in contact with my children. I had spent the crisis loan on a phone, it seemed like the sensible thing to do, needing contacts and a way of getting in touch with people on the homeless circuit as well as for the job centre. I did get one personal recognition whilst I was there from a small child around seven, a young boy with his parents walked into McDonald's behind me and went over to a table and sat down, as I walked past him he said "Hello Alan" I looked at him and he gave an exited smile and I smiled back at him and said "Hi" So it was known who I was, how they knew what I looked like I still do not know.

Craig had told me of a tent that was pitched on a mountain or large hill that wasn't being used and said to me I should stay in it as the man who owned it was in prison and wouldn't mind me using it. It sounded like a good idea and I asked him to show me where it was. It was a fair hike up the hill and at the top of it. I spent a few days in it, it was dry and out of the cold. I was still in contact with my daughter, we used to text each other now that I had a phone, things where not looking up, but they where stable. Then one early evening whilst texting my daughter I said something about her mother I shouldn't have said and we argued, I regret it to this day, I shouldn't have said it. It broke my heart when the contact ended. It was the situation and the whole mess of everything that had caused it. I upset her and wouldn't hurt her for the world. I could only hope that one day she and they would forgive me. I loved them so much. After around a week, one evening whilst I was standing outside the tent I heard a rustling coming through the woods and a man appeared, it was the owner of the tent and he didn't look very pleased at me being there. He walked over and I explained what was going on and he was alright about it, we shared the tent for the next couple of nights but it was two much, two men in a two man tent. There wasn't much room so I elected to move out and give him his space, I again slept in the alley way. I spent most days down at The Manna when it was open and Craig was good enough to let me have a shower at his flat. He was a nice guy. Then he spoke of someone called Sarah who he said may let me sleep on the floor in the living room for a few nights. Craig approached her and she agreed. I had applied for another crisis loan that would take a week or two to clear. It was £100 for a tent and a camping stove. I would pitch it on the mountain and live there for a while. Apparently no one bothered you although someone had been murdered up there a previous year. It was a chance you took. I got sort of friendly with one of the woman at the Manna and explained to her who I was and what was going on, she was telling me how much the country had changed since I was away. They had closed down all of the Tourist Information places and it was nearly summer, they where cutting back everywhere and where closing down everything with spending cuts, it was unbelievable. She politely listened to me and I actually think she believed me. After a week or so I got the letter I was expecting surrounding the loan and they had agreed to pay me £80, my state benefit had come through as well so I at last had some money in my pocket after seven years. Seven years of abject poverty and no money. It was a welcome relief. I was deciding what to do. I wasn't expecting this much at once. I could leave and go somewhere to get into a shelter, I decided I was going to leave and go somewhere else. I thought about where to go and considered Liverpool but decided that the homeless facilities there where not very good. I had experience of knowledge when I was in Liverpool sleeping in the car and there wasn't much available. I decided and was informed that Manchester was to be the best bet. I had enjoyed Kendal, the area and the people. It was a nice slow place. I had been using the library to keep the document updated and was carrying on sending it out as well as updating it.

CHAPTER 16

Manchester England

Circa March 2011

I said my goodbyes to all of the people at Manna House and walked to the bus station and waited for the bus to Manchester. It arrived and I got on, whilst on the journey I cast my mind back to all of the things that had happened to me, running around my head where many questions as to why me. What had I done, the repeated answer was nothing, absolutely NOTHING wrong. I cast my mind back to my childhood and the meeting in the dark room and the statement of "I am going to make you a saint" I couldn't figure it, was it anything to do with that? I had a feeling they where Catholic's. Had all of this stemmed from that one meeting? I would never be able to put my finger on it, though things, other things that took place in my childhood that I have still to mention at some point or place certainly did take place, this isn't even the tip of the ice berg. The miraculous events had subsided in my life now. It and they, came in fits and bursts of prophecy and happenings, but for the most part had passed. I was no longer playing games with the weather and was trying to live as normally as possible.

The bus arrived in Manchester and I got off not knowing what to do or where to go, I couldn't see any homeless out in the open. I would be sleeping on the streets until I got my bearings and found out where all of the facilities where and if there where any. I decided the best place to start was the Job centre and tell them of my new location, albeit homeless. I went in and explained the situation to them, I signed on and an interview was arranged for me. I spent the next few nights sleeping in a shop doorway in Manchester City centre. I had some money left and was eating breakfast of a morning. I looked around during the day for some cheap accommodation but there was none to be found that I could afford. I then checked on the Internet and gained the phone number of a homeless outreach centre in the city centre called Counted In. I phoned it up and they asked for the location where I was sleeping, I gave it to them, the doorway basically and they said they would come out to see me at six o'clock the following morning. That night whilst asleep in the doorway I was awoken and I was given a twenty pound note by a passing stranger, I was just about out of money now and it was welcomed. The next morning the two outreach workers woke me at 6a.m as they said they would one of them introduced himself as Tekli. They where checking I was actually homeless and telling the truth, I obviously was and they arranged a further meeting and would try to help me gain accommodation in Manchester. I had also been told about another facility in Moss Side called Cornerstone, they provided free meals and such. You could take a shower there as well. I had given the outreach workers my phone number and was waiting for a phone call from them. I then found out the exact location of Cornerstone and made my way there. It was a weekend and the facilities where not fully available so I got a sandwich and was given some more sandwiches to take away for the night. It was another Catholic facility. I left and slept back in the doorway for the next couple of nights and went back in on the Monday. On seeing me and noticing I was new they said I had to speak to one of the mental health workers as a matter of routine, I didn't like the idea born from experience but agreed. I approached him and spoke to him and gave him my name and situation, just homeless basically. I didn't tell him anything else. I think I had to sign a form or something just as some sort of statement that I had actually spoken to him. I thought no more of it. I had known from other homeless facilities that this goes on as some of the homeless have serious problems and is why they are homeless. I didn't fall into that category but had to go through the same procedure none the less. I then spoke to someone at the facility and was told that there was actually a hostel next door linked to the same facility. I walked across and knocked on the door a man I would later learn was called Lee answered the door and I asked about a room, he said they had rooms available but you needed a referral. I thanked him and left. Soon after I got a phone call from Tekli saying he would meet me at the facility the next day. I slept out again and the next day I went back. Good enough he turned up although late. I informed him that I needed a referral for the shelter next door and he said he would approach them for me. We went over and knocked and a Catholic Brother I would later know as Paul opened the door and Tekli took over and was giving me my referral. I was invited in and given a small interview in the dining room with Tekli sitting there. Paul explained the situation saying it was a Catholic hostel and that I would have to pay just over £40 per week out of my state benefit plus the housing benefit allowance of around £154. It was very expensive, nearly £200 per week but I needed the bed and agreed, telling him I was a Protestant, more than that I did not say. It was a port in a storm and I hadn't had a serious bed for over seven years. I hadn't planned on being there that long. I was later to find out it was a homeless shelter for people with alcohol problems. I was taken upstairs and shown a room and I said I would take it. It was a basic ten foot by ten foot room with a sink, a chair, a bed and a T.V. It was only going to be temporary I planned on getting a job and moving back to Liverpool to try and heal the wounds with my children. I had been taken away from them and I was hurting. Meals where provided, breakfast and evening meal. That was another bonus in spite of the cost, regular meals. I was to be left with around £30 per fortnight to spend on myself. I would be without money or much of it. But it was a start back up and out of the gutter. Brother Paul asked me if I had any clothes and I told him I had a spare pair of jeans and that was it so he went down to the outreach centre and got me a couple of pairs of socks, underpants and a clean T shirt. Over the next couple of days I went down to the housing benefit office and got my claim started and it was being processed. Tekli had also informed me that I was due a £70 clothing voucher. Everyone was entitled to it so I was due to be able to go and buy some clothes from the Primark store in Manchester when it came through.

I was there around a week when a mental health worker turned up wanting to speak to me, I asked him what it was about and he said routine. I told him I didn't have any mental health problems and had nothing to say to him. To my annoyance he then went behind my back and spoke to the brother in the office. This was my home and he had no right talking to a stranger surrounding my situation. It could have made things difficult for me especially surrounding who I am and with it being a Catholic hostel. I was very annoyed as he said I didn't have to speak to him if I didn't want to.

When my appointment was due I walked down to the Job centre for my interview and as I was walking through near the Arndale centre In Manchester city.

The phone I bought has a device on it called "Blue tooth" What it basically is, is a signal coming from your phone that enables total strangers to contact you as you walk past them within a certain distance. Bearing in mind I do not know anyone in Manchester at this point and am just paranoid about my supposed covert fame. I received a message on my phone and picked it out of my pocket to read and the message read "We hate Scousers!" I laughed and put my phone back in my pocket not replying and walked on. That is for your benefit, I already know I am famous but this isn't about fame, although sending out the document "Chasing my name globally" linked to my fame is part of it. Justice is the crux of it, the crime of gross sick perversion and life destruction, without redress or complaint or the ability to be able to say NO. I am not just saying to you "I am famous" and that is the end of it. I was being watched in my own living rooms along with my children and they had the audacity to as much as tell me they where doing it in the belief and security of an ongoing conspiracy of perversion by the entertainment industry and others. Predominantly Catholic, who gave the permission? Who gives the permission? Who decides who to choose?

I carried on walking and made my appointment to the Job centre, I had the interview and was told I would need to write or type out a C/V for my job applications I would be making, it was part of fulfilling the job seekers agreement I had signed. I had explained to them that my welding certification was no longer valid and they had been stolen anyway so getting a welding job was no longer applicable to me. I was no longer qualified. I signed on and told them I would type out a C/V for them and hand it in the next time I went in. This was going to be interesting I was going to tell the truth and I had a fair idea they where Catholics I had been interviewed by. I was polite and respectful as I always am. I went away and good enough I got to a computer and started to type out my C/V for them, within it I included the miracle and gave them my historical identity, I also explained why I had had to leave the country and was not mentally ill but stated I had been accused of it, a psychiatrist will tell you it is called a diagnosis but when you are being held and used by people who know you are telling the truth it becomes an accusation by the guilty and perverse. When I had finished it, it was two pages long, I had condensed it and cut some corners but it got the message across and you could see the truth within it. I went back to the job centre and handed it in. I had a copy of it in my email account and as part of the agreement you had to apply for something like twenty jobs every fortnight. I visited the computerised job terminals at the job centre and printed out around fifty slips of paper for jobs in local bars. I had also written a letter by hand and handed that in to some bars as well as emailing my C/V off to all of the relevant addresses I had harvested. I was fulfilling my job seekers agreement and genuinely was looking for a job behind a bar. In short I was genuinely seeking employment and wasn't playing any games, I was telling the truth to people surrounding who I was, fair enough! Between sending out the job applications I continued to harvest emails and send out the document globally. After it became obvious I wasn't going to get a reply to my C/V or the relevant job had expired and or gone I would place the email address in the document and send it out to the pub I had applied to for work. It was fair enough. I was being made covertly famous by way of "Cruel Game" and perversion. I was chasing it with evidence of same and reasoning therein. It was a spiralling nightmare.

After a couple of weeks I got a knock on my room door upstairs in the hostel and was told there was someone downstairs to speak to me. I went downstairs and walked into the dining room and the social worker / psychologist was there with another man the other man was a Pakistani in origin. They had made themselves comfortable and where sitting down at one of the tables, no appointment had been made and I wasn't notified they where coming. I stood there refusing to sit down and asked them what they wanted and the psychologist I knew, looking dirty and unshaven said to me "Let's cut to the chase and talk about the emails" I said "What?" He was trying to be very cool and it had landed on unsympathetic ears. I said I had nothing to say to them and left the dining room. I walked into the T.V lounge and made a cup of coffee feeling very annoyed at the potential confrontational attitude of them. I made my coffee and sat down to watch T.V, I then heard what sounded like their voices coming from the Brother's office and was further angered at them discussing my personal business with a complete stranger, all they where at the hostel to me where landlords and they had no right to discuss anything with them surrounding me or my sanity. It was all very underhanded and sly and I think it had stemmed from the outreach centre next door from when I had signed the forms. You will find that the Catholic's do this kind of thing. I walked up to the closed office door and knocked, hearing their voices behind it. The door opened and sure enough they where both in their talking to the brother as I suspected, I was enraged and told them so, I then asked them "What part of the word no don't you understand?!" I was furious at the arrogance of them believing they could do as they pleased with the power they had, they where destroying my life behind my back and creating atmospheres, I am a very easy going man who is very slow to anger. The Pakistani smiled nervously and they both stopped talking and left the office and then the building. Regardless of it being a homeless hostel, I was still a rent paying tenant with a right to privacy and human dignity something they had totally overlooked because of the absence of a house. They wouldn't walk up a neighbours path discussing one of the neighbours with them would they, so why do it with a landlord without a warrant or a crime committed?

A few days later I was standing on the front door step having a smoke and I recognised a man walking towards me, it was one of the police from the arrest in London, he was in plain clothes again and was with another officer, though not the same one who was present at the arrest and the woman wasn't there either. He walked up to me and said "Hello Alan you are looking a lot better, you look well!" I had put on around a stone in weight, I must have been quite thin when I arrived back in Britain, lack of food whilst living on the streets and being overactive walking everywhere etc. He immediately said that the charges against me had been dropped, I wasn't surprised at all. I didn't think it would get into a court room, with a solicitor for representation who could read and research as well as see. We spoke for a few minutes and I again addressed the situation surrounding voyeurism and perversion as well as phone tapping, I told them that what was coming out surrounding the phone tapping scandals was probably a result of that document and it didn't end there, I told them that email accounts where being broken into and monitored as well, I stated that I wanted justice and some form of compensation for what had gone on. Then the officer I hadn't seen before spoke up for the first time and asked me what I would do with justice, I said "Use it" I got the impression he was the superior. After this the first officer spoke up and said "Try not to send out to many of the documents" It was laughable. He didn't tell me not to send it out, sort of saying instead "Just send a few for us" After a few more minutes they said goodbye and left. I am still unaware as to whether they where Royal Protection Squad or just Serious Crime Squad. So, I was in the clear, someone understood it in high office probably. An accusation of mental illness was less problematic and avoided the courts. I would never again trust the police or judicial system. They can't be trusted with the truth or to uphold the law. I had explained to them once again how they are upholding the impotent Windsor's and not the law of the land. This was a criminal case they couldn't win because they where impotent evidentially, I had the evidence for it and they wouldn't accept it from a Protestant commoner who had worked miracles.

I walked along to the Job centre to sign on and an interview had been arranged, I think it was standard and nothing personal. I sat down and the woman signing officer called Helen Tickle sat down and introduced another woman who would be taking notes for her superiors, I was informed it was nothing to do with me and just for training. She started to speak and said that my C/V was to long and needed to be altered. It was only two A4 pages long and wasn't to long at all. I explained to her that I was 49 years of age and had a long work history and that I had condensed my C/V as much as I could. I became aware on later questioning that it wasn't the C/V that was the problem, it was the fact that I had made reference to a miracle and placed it in the C/V. They wanted me to take it out. I believe the signing officer was a Catholic. I had also made reference to being a Protestant within the C/V. She didn't say much more and offered the signing sheet over to me to sign, I signed it and left quite annoyed. I walked downstairs and harvested another fifty or so bar working vacancies with email addresses to fulfil my job seekers agreement. I left the building and went straight to the library at the housing office and sent out the harvested emails. To be honest with you although I was sincere about finding work and indeed working, I wasn't very hopeful it was a bit to truthful for anyone to handle. I had a few responses with a polite reply saying that the vacancy had been filled but nothing much more than that. I also got one phone call with a job offer that turned out to be a joke.

Then whilst sitting in my room again one evening at around 7p.m I got a knock at the door, it was some weeks later, I answered it and the Lee the hostel helper standing there and said that someone was here to see me in the visitors or room. I went downstairs and went to go into the visitors room and it was locked from the inside, still not knowing who it was I knocked on the door, it opened and a woman popped her head around the corner of the door peeping out, she said "Hello" and then looking back over her shoulder she said "Are we ready yet" She was actually smiling. I said "Ready for what? Who are you?" She said that they where from the mental health, I was furious, no appointments, no phone call to ask permission to come and speak to me, just a knock at the door at 7p.m at night, barging in and setting up camp in the visitors room, in my private lodgings without anyone's permission. Pig ignorance and power crazed. I then stated, not even walking into the room, that all of the charges had been dropped by the police and I had been released from the mental hospital at Hillingdon all clear. I then addressed the issue of the miracle and said I did not want to speak to them about anything. Lee stood there not saying anything but taking the situation in. I walked off and back to my room again furious at the treatment and arrogance of them. They wouldn't do this to any of the Windsor's would they!? They wouldn't get away with it. They where well over the mark.

A couple of days later I had to sign on again and when I walked in I had a different signing officer, he sat me down and stated that the C/V needed to be altered, I knew there was nothing wrong with it, I am not that bad at English and know the format a C/V takes. I had written it out correctly. I stated that I would pass a copy of it in to him the next day and he agreed and made me an appointment. I walked in the next day and after altering the C/V slightly but still leaving the bulk of it in. I stood at his desk and didn't sit down, I leaned over and said "This is my C/V There is nothing wrong with it, I am fulfilling the job seekers agreement and I have sent out at this point over one hundred applications when the required is only forty odd, the reference to the miracle stays in" People on the adjacent tables went quiet and started listening. I said nothing more and he said "Fine, no problem" and I left, there was no confrontation and I was perfectly polite but firm in my assurances. Two days later I received a letter telling me that I had been barred from the Job centre and if I was to turn up there again the police would be called and I would be arrested. I was also barred from all of the local Job centres for three months. I had done nothing. I believe it was the Catholic's panicking. I then had an eight mile round trip to the nearest Job centre I could go to, to sign on. For the first weeks I had to walk because they had caused a glitch in my payments and I never got paid. I dutifully signed on at the appropriate times and was gaining more and more email addresses to send out with my C/V and placing them in the document at a later date. I was searching for work farther afield now, all over the country with little response. I got the odd polite email refusal but that was about it. This went on for some months without further incident and I was close to being allowed back in the local Job centres and when I was I signed at another nearer Job centre than the one I had been barred from. I changed my claim basically.

I got another knock at my bedroom door and was again told there was someone to see me, I went downstairs and into the dining area and there where four people in there from the mental health. Again no phone calls, no appointments, nothing, just turning up unannounced and expecting to be seen. I had had enough, I just said "I have got nothing to say to you, all of the evidence is in the document" They hadn't even bothered to read it saying it was to long. I started to walk out of the room and was entering the hallway when the Pakistani shouted at the top of his voice and all over the house for anyone to hear "You are a paranoid schizophrenic" I opened the door of the hostel and walked out leaving them in there arriving back some time later when they had gone.

My back had been "Tweeking" for a few days and I was worried about a seizure coming up again, I had the relevant baths and it didn't seem to work I lay on the bed and that night went to sleep only to be woken some hours later in severe agony and difficulty breathing, it had effected my lungs so bad was it, I couldn't fully inflate them due to the acute pain. I couldn't move and was immobilised on the bed. I was in serious agony with breathing difficulty and couldn't ask for help as I couldn't get up off the bed. I waited until morning and somehow managed to roll off the bed and virtually on my knees go across to another resident's room and asked him to get a staff member as I was in need of an ambulance. Then Brother Brian came upstairs with a phone and I explained the situation and said I needed an ambulance. He phoned one immediately and after another phone call with me explaining to them the problem to them they turned up. I was taken to the ambulance in a chair and given a morphine injection for the pain and so I could breath. I was then taken to the hospital and went into casualty. I was there most of the day to see if the seizure subsided and was given another morphine injection, By late afternoon there was still no sign of improvement so I was admitted to the ward. Around three o'clock in the morning it had subsided enough for me to walk and I asked to be discharged but they said I needed my medication and pain killers which you could only get in the morning so I stayed in for the night walking back to the shelter the next morning, I was very much alone and felt it at this point, no one to tell, no one to phone. All I used to do, day after day, was sit in my room watching T.V, with very little money to do anything else and no where to go.

November 2011

Then one day whilst I was again sitting in my room, there was a knock at the door and Brother Brian was standing there, he said "There is someone downstairs to see you" and that is all he said. I walked downstairs and looked into the dining room and saw two woman standing there smiling, I walked farther in and then when I was all of the way in I turned slightly and saw two police officers standing there, hiding behind the door waiting for me to come in. The door was closed by one of them and I asked them what was going on. Brian the Catholic hadn't said a word about the police being their. The two women didn't say anything and just smiled, they did not know what to say. I said I had explained everything in the document and I wasn't paranoid or anything else. I informed them that I had just come out of hospital with a serious back problem and they said they already knew, they where keeping tabs on me without me knowing or being informed, how did they know? I then asked them if they had bothered to read the evidence and they said nervously that they hadn't. One of the women said "The document that is over 900 pages long" I said "Yes" She said "No" I then started to ask the police if they had read the document and they acted as if they didn't know what I was talking about. I explained to them how the Windsor's where out of their depth evidentially and that Protestants loyal to her where involved in a cover up involving what the Catholic's where doing to people and that I was being watched in my own home. Before I got much of a chance to say anything else, some sort of signal was given and I was approached by the two officers, one of them grabbed my arm and I resisted. The other one quickly came into play and I was wrestled to the floor and one of them jumped up and down on my injured back. It caused a relapse and they had done it on purpose. I had told them it was a severe back injury. I was then cuffed and as I was being led outside I said to one of the cowering woman "Are you satisfied?" as I was led outside, I then saw a waiting ambulance. I was in absolute agony as I was thrown into the waiting ambulance. Just before the doors shut one of the police officers shouted in "I am the Pope" Then made a reference to a latter part of the document, he wanted me to know he had read it. No, ill never ever trust another officer again. They had read the document and denied it. Not once was I told what was going on or the reason for the arrest. I didn't even know nor had I been told where I was going. I was just carted off. The ambulance pulled up outside Manchester Mental Health Unit, I was taken upstairs and onto the ward where the cuffs where taken off and I still wasn't informed that I had been sectioned. I received no information whatsoever, it was scary what you realise they can do to you and the power over you they have, seriously so. I was telling the truth and the Catholic's involved knew it as well as those loyal to the House of Windsor. My back was seriously bad and I was struggling to stand, they had caused serious damage to my chest as well when they jumped up and down on my back, what they did was seriously evil and purposeful, they knew the damage they where causing. I was admitted and taken to my room and I needed pain medication that was going to take some time to arrive. It was a basic room with a bed and a shower room with a toilet. I was given a nurse who would be responsible for me called Nurse Angela, she was a Catholic and I knew instantly. She told me a meeting would be arranged for me to see the ward Psychiatrist. It was to be another panel and section hearing. I didn't see the point I was already incarcerated on a lock down ward without any rights. I was given the numbers of various solicitors and phoned one up called Peter Edwards law in Liverpool. I had a vein hope that they would be able to do something. I was told that it was going to take a couple of days before they could get to me and had to accept it. I think it was the next day that Nurse Angela came up to me and said the meeting was starting soon and I said I had nothing to say to them and wouldn't be going, she then started to frighten me saying I would be forced onto medication. I was scared given what Dr Parhee had said about being strapped to the bad and drugged. The meeting had taken place without me being there, there was no point. If they where not prepared to read the evidence there was nothing I could do to save myself or them eventually. Then Angela came over to me and said it was decided that I would be taking medication, I said I wouldn't be taking anything and whilst we where talking a Dr Ashim walked past us and introduced himself as my psychiatrist. I asked when I was going to be released and he said I could go home today if I came into the office and spoke to him. I agreed and went into the office. He asked me what was going on and I started to tell him. I got to the song "Liverpool. Rotterdam, Rome" In the explanation and he went straight onto the Internet and started to research it there and then and wasn't listening, he then said if I agreed to take medication voluntarily I could go home today. I refused stating that I was not mentally ill and also stating that they had already falsified medication reports about me in Clatterbridge and the information they had on me was probably wrong and compromised. The meeting lasted no more than five minutes and I barely spoke, it was a trick to get me into the office talking to him. During all of the sections at the various mental hospitals I had no more than a total of fifteen minutes speaking. For the most part I wasn't allowed to or was being brushed off and not listened to, I had no confidence in their ability whatsoever. Angela informed me that I was under a C.T.O. a Community Treatment Order, for what I do not know. It was apparently legal. I had no rights at all. I had been stripped of them. Angela continued to pursue me and I went to my room and stayed there on the bed, I was still in agony and had been given medication that worked after a fashion, in short I was still in serious pain but it wasn't debilitating as it had been. I had informed them of how bad my back was and had severe bruising all up my arms that was to last over a week so severe was it. Nurse Angela again pursued me saying I was going to have to take medication. I got straight on the phone to the solicitors and told them of the urgency of a meeting to stop it.

They said it would take time. I contacted Peter my brother at the Daily Mirror via fax and told him of my whereabouts and the situation, I was desperate and worried. I went back to my room and lay on the bed. Some time later two women came in to check my pulse and do my heart rate and examine my injuries. They did and everything was checked out as acceptable yet I was still in serious pain. I got dressed and then a few minutes later two other women came in again with the same machine and asked similar questions, one of them asked me to drop my pants and I did. After I had, one of the women gave some sort of signal towards the door and three other women rushed in and pinned me to the bed. I was in agony and couldn't move due to my back injury. I was then injected by force with what I would later be told was Purportil or Depixol. I felt as if I had been raped. They then let me go and in severe pain I told them all to get out calling them "Disgusting bastards" I was seriously terrified now, I knew the kind of power they had, I also knew I was telling the truth and there was no convincing them in their ignorance of the game and given that Dr Ashim was a Pakistani. There would be little chance of any reasoning. His belief structure wouldn't allow it. I was told by Angela that that was the first of a series of injections to bump me up to a regular dose. I had been given 10mg and the next one would be higher. Dr Ashim came around and asked me how I was and I dismissed him. I hadn't eaten any food and wouldn't say I was on hunger strike but was refusing to eat anything, I was determined not to. This was horrendous and as alone as I have been, I have never felt more alone and vulnerable as I was right there. Peter hadn't contacted me and neither had the solicitor. It was too late. A few days later I was lying on my bed and again five nurses came in, this time one of them was a male and as they pinned me down to the bed he put his hand across my throat and was laughing at me and my position, I couldn't move, my pants where pulled down and I was again given an injection. That night I went to sleep as best as I could, I could hardly sleep but managed to get a few hours. Whilst I was asleep I felt and heard a searing and tearing inside my head and it woke me up. It was the drug I had been given. It terrified me. Where they doing any damage? I had asked one of the nurses what the drugs would do to someone who didn't have any mental problems and he said "Nothing" I wasn't so sure. I started getting movements in my legs and couldn't sit still or concentrate in one position and was constantly up and down, they where the side effects of the drug. It was causing sleep deprivation as a side effect and another one was constant movement as I have said. My back was in agony and I was on heavy pain medication for it. I would walk around the ward most of the night unable to sleep because of the drug and when I did get an hour or two I would wake up in absolute agony from my back as the drugs for it had worn off. I would then have to wait in agony in the morning for half an hour for someone to open the medical room for drugs. I hadn't told anyone I wasn't eating and at this point I hadn't eaten for over ten days only drinking coffee and no one had noticed. Dr Ashim appeared on his rounds outside my room with Nurse Angela. He asked how I was. I told him straight that the drugs where having an adverse effect on me affecting my sleep and movements, I couldn't sit still basically. He said they where side effects. I then addressed the issues again surrounding what was going on and that I wouldn't freely take any drugs from them. He said if I agreed I could return back to the hostel and go to an outreach centre for what is called a "Depot" injection. I said I was going to starve myself to death rather than take any drugs as I was sane and telling the truth, I then asked how long it would take and was told around five weeks to die from food abstention. I then addressed the question surrounding the miracle and he stated that he didn't believe in miracles, a curious statement and I reminded him that the judicial system of the country he was in was supposed to be based on that kind of truth, miracles and faith linked to nobility. I then stated it wasn't in his understanding given his belief structure. He then became visibly angry and started to posture. This was a psychiatrist unable to keep a lid on his temper in the face of a discussion surrounding my sanity. I was a Protestant standing talking to a Pakistani who's belief structure involved worshipping a woman with eight arms and an elephant, telling me he didn't believe in miracles!? I was also standing with a Catholic with a lot to cover up. I was lost. A few days later my solicitor arrived and we walked into a private room for a discussion, I felt relieved at first until she said she couldn't do anything about the use of force and the drugs administration. We discussed my situation and I went into some depth surrounding the cover up and my working a miracle in my own home. She listened politely and took some notes, but it was fairly obvious there wasn't a lot she could do, the Mental Health Authority had too much power. She said she would return in around a week, as I wasn't prepared to volunteer for drug administration she knew I would still be there. She left and I was still in no better situation. I had got some paper from the office and was keeping a diary of events. It was my only defence, telling someone the truth surrounding what was going on and it had been my only defence all along. I filled it out on a daily basis and kept a note of all of the dealings I was having with the staff and the way I was being treated. Nurse Angela came over to me one evening and handed me a letter she had written, it was her notes from the ward and she said that it was standard procedure to give the patient a copy of them. I took the notes and she walked off. As I began to read them I noticed and read that she was lying, she had said that my mental health was deteriorating and it wasn't, yes, I was having problems with the side effects from the drugs but my mental health was as sound and lucid as it had always been, she walked past me some time later and I pulled her to one side and told her she was a liar. It was bare faced lies. I then received an apology from her but it was too late, she had already filled out the form and logged it. More Catholic lies and jobs worth nest feathering off the back of my sanity. This is what you are dealing with, a stereotypical and pigeon holed accusation of insanity and the all the roads are directed down one route without any form of discussion surrounding evidence truth or proof. At that point, not one of them had bothered to read the document of evidence! I completed my diary for the day and then asked to use the fax machine to get it out to my solicitor. I was fobbed off for a couple of hours but eventually managed to send it.

One afternoon after I had been in there a couple of weeks Andy one of the helpers from the hostel came in to see me and brought in some mail. I had made photocopies of the diary I had made and handed him some copies and asked him to give one to Brother Brian to read, as I have said it included references to the miracle that took place in my own living room, I also asked him to get one to my doctor at the surgery and wanted it to go onto my medical records, I wanted some sort of record of truth in history aside from the document. I wasn't going down in history as a mentally ill nut after working miracles to cover for the ongoing Windsor conspiracy. He said he would. It was on the run up to Christmas now and I hadn't eaten for nearly twenty days I think it was, I actually wasn't hungry at all. I think it was just the situation I was in, eating was the last thing on my mind though I was drinking coffee. Still no one had noticed or picked up on it even though they fill out records of meals and where you are on the ward at certain times, I found it very lax and whilst walking around of a night, the night shift where no where to be seen. I think they where all getting their heads down somewhere. Dr Ashim again came to see me and stated that he had actually been to the hostel to see Brother Brian and was discussing me, asking as to whether I could return to the hostel?! The audacity, as I have said, all he was, was just the landlord and had no business discussing my personal matters with him. Again, you wouldn't walk up another neighbours path to discuss one of the neighbours personal business would you? I didn't like the place one bit. Soon after this I had decided that I had had enough and asked to speak to Dr Ashim, I wasn't sleeping and it was obvious that the forced drugging was going to continue and there was nothing I could do about it short of violence and I wasn't prepared to resort to that, although I did struggle as best as I could. My back had subsided a little but was still severe. When Dr Ashim turned up I informed him that if he released me I would agree to take medication, it was a nightmare. I couldn't sleep or sit still and had the shakes. He agreed to release me on the grounds that I would agree to turn up at the Kathloc Centre to receive a "Depot" injection once a month, warning me that if I refused the police would be called and I would be in there again. He then asked for my passport that I carried with me for I/D and I refused to surrender it, he then asked for the number and took it saying he was going to notify the border authorities so I could not leave the country. It was so severe and powerful. I was under threat of lock up and lock down. I was released and walked back to the hostel. No one mentioned anything about me being locked up when I returned and Brother Brian had not mentioned anything of the document or the miracle. Catholic's!? It was as if nothing had happened, no discussion, nothing.

My back was still bad and I needed medication so I went to the doctors at Boundary Lane Medical centre and saw Dr Marie. I explained the situation and she gave me some pain killers, I also told her I was having severe difficulty sleeping due to the medication and needed some sleeping tablets and she gave me those as well. I then broached the subject of my sanity and she showed me the diary I had sent her, I was relieved, she had it typed onto my file and it was there as a record. I made her as fully aware as I could in the time I had of my sanity. I then asked her for another sick note for my back injury. I had already been on the sick due to the spasm before I was carted off into the hospital. I had received a number of payments into my account whilst I was in hospital and had enough money to both pay my rent and buy a lap top computer for £140. That is what I did, I couldn't sit still long enough to use it at the desk in my room due to the drugs, it was getting bad and on my next visit to the Kathloc Centre I addressed the issue and they said they would make an appointment for me to see my psychiatrist to get the medication altered or changed. This I did and went onto, I think "Purportil" It made no difference, the side effects where just as bad and I became suicidal over it, considering taking my own life at the whole situation. I couldn't function on it at all. It was embarrassing as well, not being able to sit still anywhere I went. This went on for months, day in day out. I had been given a case worker called Sarah Barnard. She seemed nice enough and was knowledgeable at her job. She told me I would be entitled to Disability Living Allowance and filled out the relevant forms and applied for me, it was to be around £280 a month or so. I didn't like the idea as I told her I was sane and wanted a job, she was understanding but unhelpful to my cause. I then got another visit from two more Mental Health workers, again without appointment and just turning up. They where in the visitors room when I went down and I had already decided it best not to say to much to them, it just gives them fuel. They said they had come to speak to me before the section hearing and wanted to fill out some forms. I said o.k and sat and answered a few basic questions and then the male of the two, the other was a woman who sat on the other side of the room and didn't participate. He got quite aggressive saying he thought I was delusional, he was quite confrontational in his manner and I didn't rise to it. He then blurted out that my father was dead without any concern for my feelings, he didn't dress it up at all. I hadn't known. He then stated that they where unsure as to whether he was dead or not?! I was dumbfounded at his uncaring attitude. I could hardly be called delusional when the document I had sent out had made me globally famous given it went out to every nation on earth, towns cities and organisations, not just singular personal emails, but bodies and organisations. To say I was delusional at this point was ludicrous and well short of the mark and actual truth in reality. I was already famous within the organisation before I had even sent the document out! I had stopped sending the document out at this point, which is what they wanted if the truth be known. I had other things to worry about with the mental health authority, even though I was still keeping a diary of heinous events surrounding my incarceration.

Then I was called back into the Mental Health unit

for a section hearing or something, it was to be on March 8th, my birthday. I walked to the ward and waited for the pre meeting interview. After some time I was called and went into a side room near the office and sitting in there was an old Pakistani man who I found to be very arrogant. He started to question me and I was up against the same alien belief structure telling him a truth he couldn't, by definition of belief, understand. I didn't bother much and the meeting ended. I then went to the other main meeting and met my solicitor there. We went in and I stated my case but they where not interested in the truth. I was wished happy birthday and I left to stand outside the meeting whilst they discussed me. I was called back in and it had been decided that the Community Treatment Order would still be in force. I would still have to take the drugs, I was suicidal in reality. I might as well be dead for all the truth I was telling. Surely to God someone could understand this!? I left the meeting and went back to the hostel and the next time Sarah Barnard came to speak to me, she said that Dr B Ashim had left and Dr Davies was my new psychiatrists, I was relieved. I didn't know why, maybe I just didn't like the aspect of a foreign national holding me in ignorance of truth. I was called in to see Dr Davies and we had a meeting of introduction and he was the first English person I had spoken to throughout the entire saga of the Mental Health episodes. He seemed nice enough and the room was otherwise full of woman one of whom was at the computer terminal taking notes of the meeting. I explained the situation for the thousandth time and he listened, I also stated that I was in severe difficulty with the medication but didn't mention that I was suicidal through it. The meeting ended and I left. I was in a bad way with the medication, I wasn't sleeping and the sleeping tablets didn't seem to work, it was like constant sleep deprivation and it was taking its toll, I was really close to suicide now. Sarah Barnard came on her weekly meeting and check up and I addressed the situation with her stating I was close to suicide over the side effects from the drugs I was on and she arranged a meeting with Dr Davies. I turned up at the meeting and went in to the same crowd in the room and I sat in the middle of them. I addressed the situation and said I was close to suicide and if I was kept on the drugs I would take my own life, I was serious, this was horrendous. I was telling the truth and sane. Imagine sitting there telling the truth to all of these people and knowing you are sane and being forced to take drugs that are causing you to commit suicide. I was low lower than I had ever been before with nowhere to turn and no one to turn to yet again. I was asked to leave the meeting and sat outside. After around half an hour I was called back in and sat down, Dr Davies turned around and said that they where going to lift the section and I was delighted. It meant I wasn't and could not be forced to take drugs that I don't think they really know what they do to you. But, I did agree to voluntarily take a smaller dose of them for appearance sake. Thinking it wouldn't have any effect on me. Everyone was in agreement. The meeting ended and I left. Sarah Barnard was going on a course and congratulated me on my "Result" saying I would have a new mental health worker. I continued to take the Depot injection at the Kathloc centre at the reduced dosage but I still had the same results. Susan Owen my new case worker came to speak to me and I told her I would not be taking the depot injection anymore, she wasn't happy I then stated to her dismay that it had already been discussed with Dr Davies. It took around another three weeks without medication for me to reach the normality of self where I felt o.k and started sleeping properly again, the shakes had stopped and I could again function properly and once again sit still. I looked across at the lap top and decided to write to my children, this is it.

EPILOGUE

What you have just read is all true. The phone tapping scandals that have just come out in 2012 are not even the tip of the iceberg surrounding what is actually going on and the way the entertainment industry capitalised on it slightly sickened me due to their involvement in something far worse and a lot more perverse. This has been a brief insight into my life and again it is just the tip of the iceberg, there is a lot more I have not delved into. These are Elizabeth Windsor's unknown forces that they have not got the evidence of or for and as a result are covering it up either with knowledge or by definition of ignoble impotence. You are being watched in your own homes, no not all of you, people are being selected and watched. Don't tell me in this day and age it isn't possible. I have had it done to me full on for miraculous reasons. Included with that was the peripheral perversion of my children as well as various threats to them, some of which I have delved into. A lot or some of the document I have written and sent out globally has mistakes within it, as well as far too much profanity, under the circumstances of the psychological torture and perversion I have been under it is understandable. It is not just about my fame or historical placement. It is about justice and the unacceptable. I have had my entire life destroyed before Faith Country People and Family. I now live in the Catholic hostel with an eleven p.m curfew that is my prison without any hope of a future, save this story. One of the final lines of the quatrain to Cesar that states "I hope that God grants you a long life and much happiness in Felicity" Is a statement of the situation I am in now. I am in the prison of accusation and falsehoods, accused of being a paranoid schizophrenic and unable to gain employment because of it. I very rarely speak to anyone because of it and I am telling the truth. At one point the hits I was getting within and from my own living room where coming from America. A country alien to my own borders and judicial system, what you have is a situation whereby The Head of State in appearance can not admit to what they can not prove. You have a situation where the Catholic's who need the Windsor's in the palace and on their throne covering up for what they are involved in and the Protestants in "Her" ranks who are loyal to her and not justice are throwing people in mental hospitals who are complaining about it or saying it is going on. If you are not me and have not worked a miracle to at least give you a chance of proving it you are lost, they will destroy your whole life without the blink of an eye or the bat of an eye lid, you'll get laughed at and ridiculed by the Protestants loyal to her whilst it is being done. There is a massive "Game" going on surrounding it and this, it involves serious perversion and soul theft, they are taking your life. They have made Millions and Millions and Millions and then some out of my life alone both musically and politically and in the cold light of day and truth I am an incredibly globally famous man and real, with historical placement and the necessity for proving it for the sake of the rest of my Faith, in short I do not have a choice. I am at this point now 49 years of age and unable to form a relationship with another woman because of untrue allegations of insanity. I have very little money or prospects of a future and can not get any form of legal representation or compensation for this heinous perverted and sick crime because the solicitors and legal world, inclusive of complicit judges are all connected to an impotent crown and Bar that is flawed evidentially and is ignoble. It could also be argued that the Windsor's are not even British without lineage, Albert was a German and Philip was a Greek. So to say there is national justice or justice in any guise of right and truth is laughable in light of evidence. To admit that I am telling the truth is to admit to impotence treason and ignobility. In short there is no justice and it is understandable in explanation. They are not the Heads of State or the Protestant Faith and never can be in light of this evidence. If you find yourself in receipt of evidence of a crime involving the Catholic Church you don't get back up, you get stabbed in the back, you can not go to the police or gain legal representation, it becomes clear that it is that very fact that they bank on, a crime of impunity. The greater the evidence you have the less chance you have of gaining justice and if your evidence involves a miracle you are finished and doors are slammed in your face. For me, working that miracle in my own living room and home and catching them doing it was like buggering the Bishop. What should have been a Historic event became a very embarrassing moment for them. I was as much as forced onto the street because of it and had my entire life destroyed along with any relationship with my children. I now undergo constant monitoring by the mental health authorities to the point of persecution. I am constantly asked the same questions time and time again, giving the same answers time and time again, both lucid, placid and sane. To say I am not angry by this wouldn't be true, I am but to lose my temper is to fall into the "Told you so" trap. Once they get a grip of you, the power they wield over you in the forceable drugging sense is scary. They can invade your life and go around behind your back questioning people and insinuating. The very introduction of "I am from the mental health" rings alarm bells. Something they have no care about, they trample in and around your private life without care and or abandon. You have no redress for it or complaint or you are further accused, it is a vicious circle and they do all of this with a smile on their face. It is there for the rest of your life, on records, documentation and in history and they are set aside from the judiciary and pig ignorant of truth or about game and conspiracy. I firmly believe that had I not have put that advert in the Liverpool Echo for a Managers Job as a dated historical fingerprint in the press, I would not be alive today to tell you this. I could quite easily of gone missing and no one would have been any the wiser as to my identity or history, there would just have been a gap in history that no one could or would explain.

The Protestant Faith spans more than the borders of this country so to say that I am an English Protestant, whilst true, it goes a lot deeper when you consider what the Catholic church are involved in. In short I have a duty of getting this evidence out given identity historic. Irrespective of accusation the reasoning's for, now clear. I am typing this out on a closed computer lap top and although I am not that computer literate I am fairly sure it is secure. I have not got it connected to the Internet and don't think anyone can break into it to tamper with the Document /Book.

Elizabeth Windsor and co. If I can not get this published, either none fiction or indeed fiction, I am going to get it printed out myself and hand it out to Protestants who I do not think are involved in this and who don't or didn't know it was going on. You have not got the evidence to prove it, I have. I am not mentally ill. I was being watched in my own home as was Diana Spencer who was also sane and lucid. It makes your skin crawl. I have worked miracles, which is obviously a major problem for you and the complicit judiciary given my lineage and faith.

THE WHOLE THING STINKS

Lightning Source UK Ltd.
Milton Keynes UK
UKHW01f0630030518
322038UK00001B/95/P